The Love of
TROPICAL FISH
Freshwater & Marine

The Love of TROPICAL FISH
Freshwater & Marine

Keith Sagar with Jack Swain

octopus

CONTENTS

Introduction

Nearly all the permanent waters of the world, still or moving, salt or fresh, are stocked with fishes, over 20,000 species of them. The greatest proliferation of species and the most exotic of them are found in the lakes and ponds, swamps, streams, rivers, estuaries and coral seas of the tropics. Most of the species of freshwater tropicals commonly kept by aquarists come from South America, Africa and South East Asia; most of the marine species from the Pacific and Indian Oceans and the Caribbean.

The majority of nature's beautiful creatures are seen at their best at liberty in their natural surroundings. If we look at mammals or birds in cages, we know that this is a poor substitute. However healthy and well-cared for they may be, captivity takes the bloom from their beauty, constricts their vitality and compromises their dignity. This is true also, to a degree, with fishes – nothing is more pathetic than a blank-eyed goldfish swimming round and round an otherwise empty bowl: there is no excuse for that. But fishes, being water creatures, not of our element, are very difficult to see in their natural surroundings, and often, in any case, show little of their colour there. And

Endpapers: Harlequins *Rasbora heteromorpha*
Half Title: Thick-lipped Gourami *Colisa labiosa*
Title page: Blue Moon Angelfish *Pomacanthus maculosus*
Contents page: Banded Pipefishes
Below: Neon Tetras *Paracheirodon* or *Hyphessobrycon innesi*
Left: Tomato Clowns *Amphiprion frenatus* with sea anemone

8

they are small enough for it to be practicable for us to recreate their homes within our own, to make a miniature underwater world, a complete ecological system, with animals, plants and minerals in a balanced relationship. With no other creatures can this be so easily achieved. There is no smell, no mess, no prohibitive expense, and infinite possibilities for imagination and creativity, for breeding and exhibiting and photography.

Fishes were kept as pets in China a thousand years ago. The first book on fish-keeping, Chang Chi-en-te's *The Book of the Vermilion Fish* appeared in the sixteenth century. Chang described the beauty of his pet, how he fed it, and mentioned its reaction to temperature changes. In 1665 Pepys mentioned in his diary:

'My wife and I were shown a fine rarity: of fishes kept in a glass of water, that will live so for ever; and finely marked they are, being foreign.'

It is impossible to guess what they might have been, and whether or not they were tropical. A century later the keeping of goldfishes in ponds or bowls had become a common practice in England. The concept of a 'balanced' aquarium was first put forward by A.W.T. Brande in 1819. In his book *A Manual of Chemistry* he described the way in which living plants reoxygenate water, so that an aquarium could be set up which would not need water changes. Philip Gosse founded the world's first public aquarium at London Zoo in 1853, and the following year

wrote a book on fish-keeping in the home. A decade later came the first certain importation of a live tropical fish to Europe – the Paradise Fish (*Macropodus opercularis*), a very attractive and hardy fish which is still kept by European aquarists.

The next major advance was the principle of circulating water with pumps, a method invented by English

Left: Rainbow Butterflies *Chaetodon trifasciatus*
Above: Regal Angel *Pygoplites diacanthus*
Right: Anglerfish *Antennarius* sp.

aquarists but first put into operation at the Paris aquarium opened in 1860. The Hamburg and Berlin aquariums also opened in the 1860s.

All three had seawater tanks, and the Berlin aquarium was the first to use artificial seawater. The Germans rapidly took the lead in all branches of the subject. Their scientists were the first to organize expeditions to find and classify new species. Their traders were the first to open up collecting stations and ship tropical fishes in large quantities to Europe and America. Their amateur hobbyists were the first to discover how to breed many species in captivity.

But it is only in the last fifty years that tropical fish-keeping has developed into the popular hobby it is today. Since the Second World War, air transportation and large-scale commercial breeding have brought prices down and led to a boom in the hobby. Singapore is probably the fish centre of the world, with its ideal climate. Fish farms there produce millions of fishes each month for distribution to all parts of the world. There are thousands of small fish farmers all over the Malay Peninsula who dig shallow fish pools wherever they can afford the space, introduce a few pairs of fishes and some commercially popular plants and leave nature to do the rest. Or they utilize the rice paddies in the same way. There are very large, highly commercialized fish farms in Florida. In Japan, a large industry has grown up breeding the cold-water species, such as goldfishes and carp of fantastic shapes and colours. In Hong Kong, breeders have mastered some of the most difficult species, such as Neon Tetras, and are now breeding them on a commercial scale.

Hundreds of species are now kept in home aquariums and many are bred there. Moreover, aquarists have 'created' countless new varieties and transformed many only moderately attractive species into quite beautiful creatures. The humble Guppy (*Poecilia reticulata*) is the most remarkable example. Nature provided the diminutive male Guppy with splashes of several colours, but he was more like a palette than a painting, until selective breeding produced the many gorgeous varieties of fancy Guppies we know today.

Some species have been seriously depleted by overfishing to supply the hobby; but others threatened by pollution or the destruction of habitats are safe from extinction because of the large breeding stocks held in captivity. This applies only to freshwater species. Marine tropicals cannot yet be bred in captivity. Much attention is being devoted to the problem, and a breakthrough may not be far away. But we are running out of time. In the interests of conservation the present uncontrolled pillaging of the reefs (for corals and shells as well as for living specimens) cannot be allowed to continue.

Right: Moorish Idol *Zanclus canascens*
Below: Green Swordtails *Xiphophorus helleri*

Freshwater Tropical Fish
in the Home Aquarium

There is no limit to the ingenuity of aquarists and almost anything that will hold water has been at one time or another converted into an aquarium. Old television sets and beer barrels have been adapted with great skill, but they, together with the more conventional metal-framed aquariums are now somewhat old hat – we have arrived at the plastic age. The beginner with limited capital is well provided for with a first-class range of relatively inexpensive one-piece plastic aquariums supplied complete with condensation tray and canopy. Whilst these are more easily scratched than glass, they have the virtue of being almost unbreakable in normal conditions and they do not leak. Those who can do so, however, are recommended to consider the installation of an all glass aquarium with a capacity of at least twenty gallons. The frameless, all-glass tank is made possible by the development of silicone-based rubber sealants of great strength and dependability. Rusting frames and leaking tanks (with consequent electrical hazards) need be tolerated no longer.

There is now greater flexibility in design than ever before, since all-glass tanks can be made in almost any conceivable shape. They are neat enough to be attractive with only a canopy and stand, or they can be housed in custom-built cabinets to match the furnishing of the rooms for which they are intended. A well constructed, arranged and maintained aquarium can be the centre-piece in the decor of a room. In a room without a fireplace, an aquarium makes an excellent alternative focal point. On the other hand, an aquarium which has been badly set up or allowed to run down can be an eyesore.

Depth adds greatly to the aesthetic effect of an aquarium, but remember that if your tank is more than two feet deep you will not be able to reach the bottom and that will be a great inconvenience.

The siting of the aquarium is important, for both aesthetic and operational reasons. It would, for example, be a mistake to position the aquarium where direct sunlight falls on it for any length of time. The fishes would have no objections, but the tank would soon be choked with unsightly algae. On the other hand, if the tank is placed in a dark spot it will enhance the surroundings and the artificial lighting can be operated in such a way as to

Lace Angels *Pterophyllum eimekei*, Scats *Scatophagus argus*, *Metynnis schreikmuelleri*

13

control any unwanted and unnecessary plant and algae growth.

The condition of the water is of fundamental importance. Temperature, clarity, pH value (loosely referred to as acidity or alkalinity), hardness, colour and oxygen content are perhaps the most important properties. The greatest problem is that created by the aquarist himself when, in his enthusiasm, he seeks to keep a wide variety of fishes in the same tank. Many of these may have originated from very different environments and it is all too often difficult for them to thrive in the same conditions. In community tanks a whole series of compromise conditions must be created if reasonable success is to be achieved. Water temperature should be 75 °F. (23.5 °C.) though Mountain Minnows are happy at much lower temperatures and Discus at much higher.

The term pH denotes the degree of acidity and alkalinity of the water. The pH is expressed in a scale of numerical values on either side of 7 which is neutral.

Solutions are increasingly acid as the value falls below 7 and alkaline as the value rises above it. There are many simple and reliable kits on the market which enable accurate pH control to be maintained. They consist of a colormetric scale together with buffering solution. Unless the aquarist intends to specialize in particular species, the best compromise is 6.9 (slightly acid) for a community tank. There are, of course, exceptions. Black Mollies, for example, can live and breed quite happily in a pH of 8.3 whereas the Neon Tetra and the Killifishes are quite at home in pH values of around 6.0 or even lower. Frequently (though not invariably) there is a relationship between pH value and hardness of water.

The hardness or softness of water is related to the amount of calcium dissolved in it. The more calcium, the harder the water. Here again the optimum hardness or softness varies with the species of fish being kept, but speaking in general terms most fishes do best in a relatively soft water and are affected adversely by a high calcium content. The exceptions are the Mollies and most brackish-water fishes, such as Scats and Malayan Angels which require hard water with a high specific gravity.

Water colour (not to be confused with clarity) often depends on whether or not carbon is included in the filter bed and may often be affected by the intensity of the aquarium lighting. Tinting of water occurs primarily when conditions in the aquarium become unbalanced. A green tinge is developed when excessive light is present which is responsible for the uncontrolled growth of algae. There are several conditions which generate a brown tinge but perhaps the most common is lack of light coupled with plant decay. The presence of wooden decor components or peat substances may also be a cause. Clarity can be restored quite easily by filtering the water through activated carbon.

Filtration is, without doubt, fundamental to successful fish-keeping. Any consideration of the topic of filters is complicated by the fact that there are almost as many types as there are days in the year. Probably the simplest and cheapest are best. The undergravel filter plate provides a perforated floor on which the gravel lies. Water from the aquarium passes through the gravel, through the perforations of the plate and is then hoisted back into the aquarium with the aid of an air lift tube. This constant filtration process is relatively simple mechanically but in terms of chemical changes it is complex and fascinating. The question in the mind of most enquirers is, 'Whatever happens to the dirt?' And the answer is a fairly simple one – it is 'digested' in the gravel. As the water passes through the gravel bed it brings a constant supply of oxygen with it and this fosters the growth of aerobic bacteria on the gravel surfaces. Waste matter or 'dirt' carried with the water coming into contact with the aerobic bacteria is broken down into its simpler components and thus converted into gas(es), water, soluble mineral salts and a small amount of residue called mulm. Very little maintenance is necessary. All that is required is that the gravel should be thoroughly agitated or stirred every few months in order to release the accumulated mulm and this can be removed by the simple process of syphoning off.

The filter plate should cover most of the base of the aquarium. The throughput rate should be adjusted so that the total volume of water passes through the system every two hours. Real advantages of this simple filtration system are that so little of it need be visible, and that it needs little or no maintenance.

The commonest alternative internal filter is the box type. All box filters operate on the same principle, that of passing the water through a disposable medium of one kind or another. Examples of the mediums used are filter wool, carbon, gravel, etc. In the case of filter wool it must be appreciated that we are not referring to ordinary cotton wool which would, if used, result in heavy organic pollution, but to a special non-organic material made from synthetic fibre. Glass wool should be avoided, it is dangerous material to play around with. The latest form of wool filter is in the form of a mat, which has been woven into a flat sheet and can be cut to any size, washed when necessary and re-used. Activated carbon (made from bone or shell) is the best type, and will produce crystal-clear water; but it does tend to neutralize the pH and is therefore not suitable if acid water is required. Carbon should be renewed about every three months.

'Hook on' external box filters are available in both power and air lift forms. The aquarium water is drawn by a syphon technique into the chamber, the motor or

Left: Jewel Cichlid *Hemichromis bimaculatus*
Above: Ram *Apistogramma ramirezi*

airlift pumping the filtered water back into the aquarium. The power filter is operated by an electrically driven water impeller and consists basically of the filter box and motor unit connected to the aquarium by means of flexible hose. Earlier models created problems related to failure of hose connections and flooding created by faulty water-flow control; the units now in production are of high quality and dependability – accidents are rarely encountered. The filter medium is of the same kind as used in internal filters but the turnover rate is of course very much greater and the electric motors used are so quiet that they are practically inaudible. All in all they really do enhance the quality of aquariums and convert the ordinary to the luxurious not only in function but in appearance also.

Temperature control of the aquarium is of course an essential aspect of successful operation; reliable equipment is desirable and it is most unwise to purchase cheap or shoddy equipment when the health or even the lives of your fishes depend to a great extent on it. For many years past aquarists have been using combined heater/thermostats. These have the distinct advantage of having only a single electric lead from the aquarium and the user cannot therefore accidentally overload the thermostat. Many an accidental 'boiling' has occurred because of wiring several relatively high-powered heating elements to a single small thermostat which was unable to cope with the load it was asked to carry. The power or strength of heaters used in aquariums should be just adequate to maintain the required temperature in the coolest conditions envisaged. The idea of having plenty of power to spare is not a good one. A further precaution well worth taking is to place the heating element just immediately above the gravel; this ensures that the entire volume of water in the tank is heated even if the filtration and aeration processes fail. It is worth mentioning too that the heater should never be switched on unsubmerged; it is likely to overheat and crack the tube. Thermostats, too, are many and varied but there is only one type other than the internal which is in common use – the external 'clip on' type, usually incorporating a warning light and adjustment control. There is a heavy duty model too, specially designed to take several heaters with safety. It is possible to use one such thermostat to control several tanks providing of course that the power of the heaters is proportionate to the capacity of the tanks. It is highly desirable for all aquariums to have cover glasses or condensation shields in order to prevent moisture coming into contact with light fittings or even with the canopy itself. One quite popular type of aluminium canopy is designed to function without a cover glass but this is dangerous both electrically and chemically – aluminium oxides can contaminate the water, and in the case of a marine tank this can be fatal for both fishes and invertebrates.

Lighting deserves careful attention not only for the added aesthetic pleasure it may give but because fishes need it and it is essential to plant growth. A basic guide to the inexperienced would be that a forty watt bulb or tube eighteen inches above the gravel will be adequate for an area of two square feet, if in operation approximately ten hours a day. Space-age technology must be thanked for giving us fluorescent tubes specially designed to promote plant growth. These also enhance the colours of the fishes, especially blue and red. The higher initial cost of these tubes is more than compensated for by the longer life and lower running cost.

What you do with the back of the aquarium can make or mar the whole effect. If you paint it you cannot change your mind. Colour reproductions of thickly planted tanks can be placed behind the back glass. Sheets of blue or green plastic can be bought which have the advantage that they can be placed inside the tank to hide all air-lifts and heater wires. Or an illusion of great depth can be created by placing a pale-blue background some distance behind the tank or placing the tank with its back to a window, and sticking to the outside of the back glass a sheet of translucent blue or green protective film such as is sold for covering books and documents. If there is space behind the tank, corals and sea-fans can be placed there to add to the optical illusion of extreme depth.

Gravel is normally used as compost and is preferable to the artificial and often garishly coloured composts on sale. Let the fishes and plants provide your bright colours. The gravel should be thoroughly washed several times, then spread over the filter plates to a depth of two inches at the front and three to four inches at the back. The filter plates should be placed away from the back and sides of the aquarium to allow for the planting of deep-rooted plants there, which would otherwise have all the sustenance drawn away from their roots by the filter.

Next, position the rocks. These should not be so large as to take up most of the swimming space, nor so jagged that fishes might injure themselves against them. Water-smoothed rocks taken from a river bed are best.

To introduce corals and sea shells into a freshwater tank for decoration would be courting disaster because the calcium content of the shells or coral would slowly affect the degree of hardness and pH of the water. The same rule should be applied to any form of marble, or such rocks as limestone or tufa which are both high in calcium. Suitable rocks include sandstone, granite, quartz and slate. All stones should be of the same type. Small rocks or chippings placed at the foot of the larger pieces

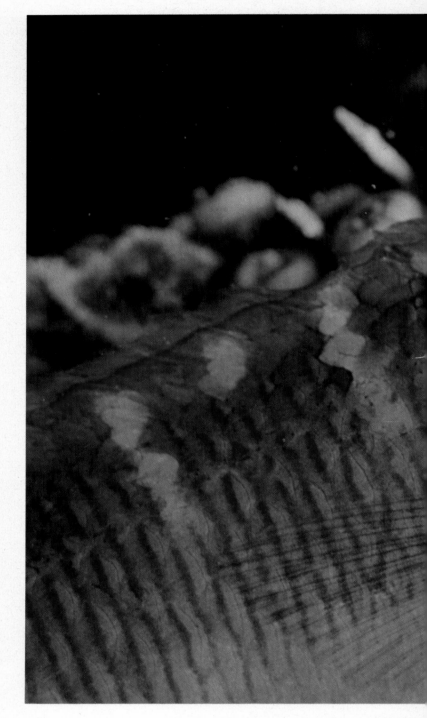

look well. If stratified rock is used a much more natural effect is obtained by making sure that the strata all run at the same angle, preferably horizontal or just slightly tilted. The base of the rocks should be buried in the gravel to give the impression that only the tips of great slabs are visible. In addition to rocks, gnarled roots or pieces of thoroughly saturated bogwood can be used as decor. These can often be found or bought in grotesque shapes.

When the gravel and rocks are in position, half fill the tank, pouring the water gently on to a sheet of paper or plastic or floating board to avoid disturbing the gravel. Install your heaters at this stage and test them (making sure they are fully submerged). You are now ready to begin planting.

Plants are virtually essential, both aesthetically and biologically, for the freshwater aquarium. Fishes take in oxygen and give out carbon dioxide. Plants do the reverse. With too many fishes and too few plants the build-up of carbon dioxide could become lethal. In any

Lyretail Wrasse *Thalassoma lunare*

case, there is no more attractive way of decorating a tank than with natural plants and rocks.

Most aquariums are too thinly planted. If you cannot see the back of the tank for plants, so much the better. You have got too many plants only when you cannot see the fishes. The tallest and thickest plants should be placed along the back and sides of the tank, particularly in the back corners where they can be used to hide air-lifts and heaters. Vallisneria is suitable for this purpose or such fine-leaved vigorous plants as Cabomba or the fern-leaved plants such as Ceratopteris (Indian Fern) or Wisteria. In front of these, given plenty of room, can be the broad leaved feature plants such as Aponogeton, Echinodorus (Sword plants), Hygrophilia, Ludwigia, and the larger Cryptocorynes. In the foreground can be planted the smaller Cryptocorynes, Hairgrass and the various pigmy plants such as *Nymphaes x daubenyana*, a tiny Waterlily. If your aquascape requires the planting of some plants over the filter-plates, small plantpots can be used, which must,

of course, either be buried or hidden by rocks.

When you are satisfied with your aquascape, fill the tank to the desired height, and leave it with all the systems running for a few days before adding fishes.

There is, of course, no need to have the aquarium entirely filled with water. Surface area is more importance than gallonage, and a partially filled tank offers great opportunities to the imaginative aquarist for creating a sense of the continuity between the life of a stream or river or lake and that of its banks. Many exotic plants grow at the water's edge and many aquatic plants bloom above the surface.

The purist would argue that, since his aim is to bring a little section of aquatic nature into his home, he must restrict himself to fishes which actually are found living together, perhaps even to a shoal of a single species,

Above: Harlequins *Rasbora heteromorpha*
Below: Silver Hatchets *Gasteropelecus levis*
Right: Platy *Xiphophorus maculatus*

together with plants which would form their natural habitat. Though most aquarists would not wish to go as far as that, there is no denying that shoals do look much more attractive than mixed collections, and that large clusters of a few species of plants look better than individual specimens or small clumps of many.

Let us assume for the moment that the aquarist who has just set up his first tank cannot resist the temptation to keep a wide range of species in it. He should not be too impatient to buy, but should read several books and talk to several experienced aquarists and dealers.

Do not overcrowd your tank. One inch of fish to each gallon is enough. Obviously fishes which are large enough to eat or aggressive enough to damage other fishes must be avoided. You cannot, for example, keep large cichlids if you intend also to keep any small fishes at all. Tiger Barbs will frequently nip the fins of other fishes, though they are less likely to do this if you have a shoal of them than if you have only one or two. Some fishes, Tinfoil Barbs for example, will quickly strip all your plants. Water which is soft and acid enough to suit tetras, dwarf cichlids and gouramis, is unlikely to suit mollies, scats or Malayan Angels.

The habits of fishes should be taken into account. Cat-fishes and loaches stay on the bottom and are useful

scavengers. Hatchets and Half-beaks stay on the surface. The shape of your fishes is also important where the overall aesthetic effect is concerned. Most of your fishes will be torpedo-shaped. It is effective to have a few fishes of other shapes to contrast with these – angels, hatchets and fighters, for example. A few slow-moving fishes, fighters or cichlids, will contrast with the quicksilver danios or rasboras. A few black fishes, mollies or Black Veiltail Angels will again make a dramatic contrast with their brightly coloured tank mates.

Single specimens never look as good as pairs, nor pairs as good as shoals, where a shoaling species is concerned. Why not buy a small shoal, ten or twelve specimens of your favourite shoaling fish, then just add a few other species to contrast with them in appearance and behaviour. Some fishes such as White Cloud Mountain Minnows or Harlequins or any of the barbs or danios, which may not be particularly spectacular or interesting as individuals, acquire a new magic when a small shoal of them gracefully swim as one across a spacious tank against a background of luxurious vegetation.

Each aquarist will soon discover his own favourites (and must learn to be tactful when shown someone else's favourites, which leave him cold). I can only say what, for me, would constitute an ideal community for a

fifty-gallon tank: ten or twelve Cardinals, ten or twelve Harlequins, two Black Veiltail Angels, two Leopard Catfishes, two Marbled Hatchets, a pair of fancy guppies, a pair of Hi-fin Swordtails, one male Pearl Gourami, one male Siamese Fighter, one male *Apistogramma ramirezi*.

The majority of beginners tend to over- rather than under-feed. Uneaten food settles on the bed of the aquarium and is quickly covered in fungus. Any sign of cottonwool-like growth on the gravel is a strong indication of gross overfeeding. The fishes should consume all the dry food added to the tank within five minutes, otherwise they will lose interest. Four basic types of food are available: dried, freeze dried, fresh and live. The most popular of the dried foods is in flake form; it contains all the basic necessities and has vegetable matter, proteins, carbohydrates, minerals and fats in its composition. Many brands are available and the dependability and standard of most is very high. There are still many advocates of the types of food which were common some years ago, foods such as ant eggs, mosquito larvae, dried daphnia and the like, but it is doubtful whether the fishes receiving the food share the enthusiasm of their keepers. The accelerated freeze-drying process in its essential elements consists of deep freezing at very low temperatures and applying a vacuum; temperature is then raised slightly which causes

Above: Giant Gourami *Colisa fasciata*
Right: Silver Hatchet *Gasteropelecus levis* with Marbled
Hatchet *Carnegiella strigata*

the phenomenon of water 'boiling off' well below freezing level. When the food is put in water it is reconstituted in virtually the same form as before freeze-drying.

Former dehydrating methods left dried-up shells and little else. F.D. (freeze dried) daphnia or tubifex worm reconstitutes into a perfect food almost as good as 'live' would be. Artemia or Brine Shrimp is now freely available in F.D. form and is suitable for fishes of all types. By fresh food is meant scraped raw meat (especially liver) and fish.

Nothing we have said should prevent the keen aquarist from providing live food when it is clean and available. All fishes naturally prefer it. Most dealers sell live daphnia, tubifex, glassworm and bloodworm, or the aquarist can catch his own daphnia in a local pond. Daphnia or water-

fleas are actually fresh-water crustaceans about the size and shape of fleas but not, of course, related to them. They will almost always be found together with their smaller relative, cyclops, which is just as good for food. Tubifex worms are harvested from mud-banks in rivers. They will stay alive for weeks under a dripping tap. Dealers also sell starter-cultures of whiteworms (Enchytrae). These are kept in small boxes of damp earth with a piece of glass resting on the surface of the soil. They are fed on pieces of brown bread soaked in milk. They will breed if not too hot or cold (the cupboard under the sink is a good place). They gather in knots around the bread and on the cover-glass and can easily be removed with tweezers for feeding. When a small earthworm is thrown into an aquarium of fishes which may never before have seen one, interest is created even in the most reluctant feeder. The messy business of chopping the worm up into suitable small pieces is of course a necessary preliminary. A recent development is vitamin supplements in tablet or powder

form. Although they are not strictly foods they are well worth using occasionally.

In the case of accidental overfeeding we are confronted with the problem of efficiently 'cleaning' the aquarium. An ordinary syphoning technique with flexible tube and bucket may be used, but beware of drawing fish into the tube. Many types of small under-water vacuum cleaners are available operated by electric motor or air pump. These will draw the mulm or floating debris into a collecting bag thus allowing the filtered water to pass back into the aquarium. It will also be necessary to change up to 25% of the water. This should be done, in any case, about once a fortnight. Tap water is rarely if ever similar in character to 'aged' aquarium water and if a change can be foreseen it is worthwhile to collect rain water, which must of course be clean. It is quite a simple matter to tie a plastic bag to a downspout (after letting the initial flow wash dust or dirt) and water collected can be stored in any suitable plastic container until required.

Should algae build up on the internal glass surfaces suitable scrapers made from plastic or hard rubber as well as sponges and razor-blade holders are available, but never use the razor-blade scraper on a plastic aquarium. Or there are magnetic cleaners which enable one to clean the glass on both sides without so much as removing the canopy or rolling up one's sleeves. The novelty value of this device is such that volunteers for glass cleaning are never scarce.

Careful observation of the behaviour patterns of the fishes – their feeding habits, breathing rate, swimming movements and attitudes to other fishes will tell you of impending trouble. Any deviation from normal will be conspicuous. They can be watched carefully for symptoms of disease and treated in good time. Changes are not always due to illness or water conditions. Fishes coming into breeding condition can often be very aggressive. When you switch on a light in a dark room, many fish will have lost all their colour and be sitting on the bottom of the tank. Within a few minutes they regain their colour and start to swim about again.

Illness will often show when a fish swims with closed fins, becomes listless, breathes heavily and loses colour during the day. Sometimes there are external symptoms in the form of white spots or fungus growth and this of course must be treated. When making diagnosis of illness always have regard to three basic possibilities (i) it can be a disease, (ii) it can be a difficulty related to water conditions, or (iii) it can be a difficulty related to community tank compatibility.

So far as water condition is concerned, a check should be made in respect of temperature, aeration, filtration, pH value and possible sources of contamination such as paint fumes, insect or deodorant sprays, or tobacco smoke. The risk of pumping contaminated air into the tank can be avoided by placing the pump in some infrequently-used room where the air is fresh and clean, or even under the floorboards or in the garage. Even small pumps will blow air along many yards of airline if kinks are avoided.

Having eliminated water conditions or incompatibility as the cause of abnormal fish behaviour the hobbyist is left with the possibility of disease or illness, and the more obvious ailments should be looked for first. 'White Spot' is the commonest of fish diseases and is not always obvious or easy to see. The small white parasite spots usually appear first on the transparent areas of the fins and subsequently on the body. This is a contagious disease and early diagnosis and treatment is most advantageous. Several excellent cures are available of Malachite Green, which does not require the inconvenience of changing temperatures or altering the lighting routine of the aquarium. It will seldom do any harm to treat for White Spot when fishes are ill from something which cannot be diagnosed. There are many variations of this disease such as Velvet or Dust which respond to the same treatment.

Fin-rot and fungus are fairly easy to identify. Most of the common fungus infections can be cured by the addition of common salt to the water, but in stubborn cases the fish can be dipped in a fungus cure in the form of a dye which continues to work after the fish has been replaced in the aquarium.

Gouramis often develop dropsy which causes swelling to an extent in which the scales protrude from the body. Unfortunately there seems to be no easy cure for this disease and it is often kinder to destroy the affected fish.

Less common diseases occur which need specialist advice one of which is parasitic gill flukes; this condition yields to treatment with a mild acid: a teaspoonful of vinegar to a cup of aquarium water will cause the flukes to detach themselves.

Whatever problems related to disease may occur we strongly advocate reference to specialized literature. The hobbyist should not allow himself to be panicked into taking hasty actions which are irreversible before being reasonably sure of the nature of the problem.

One of the major advantages of freshwater fishes in comparison with marines is that they can be bred by the amateur aquarist, even by the absolute beginner. Indeed where live-bearers are concerned it is only necessary to put a male and a female in the same tank and they will do the rest. From there the aquarist can progress to more and more difficult species until, perhaps, he reaches those frontiers of the hobby where he applies himself to species not yet spawned or reared in tanks. Even then he is not likely to forget the day he first saw a minute pair of black eyes swimming on the surface of his tank – his first baby Guppy.

Methods of breeding differ so greatly from one family of fishes to another, or even from one species to another, that it will be easier to discuss them in the relevant chapters.

Blond Guppies *Poecilia reticulata* (below: female, right: male)

The Fishes

FAMILY POECILIIDAE
Live-bearing Toothed Carps

This family originates from Central and South America. It includes Guppies, mollies, Swordtails, Platies, Half-beaks and a few other little-known species. They vary in size from the Mosquito Fish which is less than an inch long to the Giant Sailfin Molly which can reach six inches. The life-span is from two to five years depending on size. In the aquarium they prefer well-matured, slightly alkaline water, but they are very tolerant. They are surface-feeding fishes with a wide diet which includes green food and live food. In the aquarium they will eat whatever is offered. They are peaceful in a community tank. They breed more freely than any other tropical fishes. In short, they are the ideal fish for the beginner.

The common name refers to the fact that live-bearers do not, like the vast majority of fishes, lay eggs, but give birth to free-swimming young.

For this reason they were long regarded as freaks of nature, like the Duck-billed Platypus, a mammal which lays eggs. In fact, there is little similarity between the reproductive systems of live-bearing fishes and mammals. The fertilized egg is simply kept within the female's body until it hatches.

At no time is the baby attached to the mother's blood-stream or dependent on her for food as in the mammal. Nor is there anything to compare with the maternal instinct in mammals. On the contrary, the live-bearing mother is likely to swallow her babies at one end as fast as they emerge at the other.

It is very easy to distinguish the sexes in this family. The female has a full, triangular anal fin, whereas that of the male is modified to the shape and function of a penis. The male is usually smaller than the female and more brightly coloured. The sexual drive is very strong in the male, who pesters the poor female ceaselessly. It is therefore good practice to have several females to each male, especially since one fertilization can

Right: Snakeskin Guppy *Poecilia reticulata*
Far right: Snakeskin Guppy *Poecilia reticulata*
Below: Multi-coloured Guppy *Poecilia reticulata*

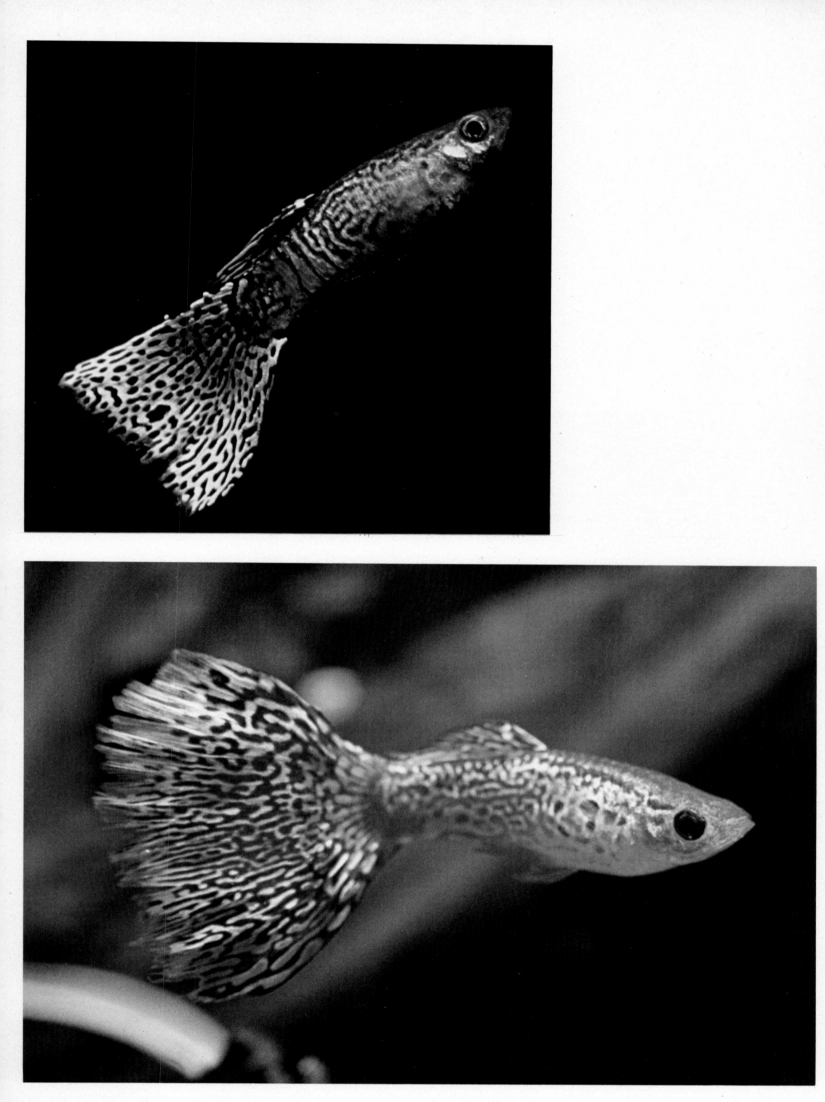

frequently sire three or four broods.

Females mature early and can reproduce at about four months. A mature female can drop a hundred or more babies at intervals of four or five weeks. The eyes of the unborn young are often visible as a 'gravid spot' near the anal fin of the mother. This is at its largest and darkest just before she gives birth. To save the young it is best to put the gravid female into a breeding trap, a device designed to allow the babies to fall through a small aperture into a nursery compartment where they will be safe from predators.

The Guppy (*Poecilia reticulata*) is named after Dr. R. Guppy who first collected it in Trinidad in 1866. It is probably the world's most popular tropical fish, and it is not difficult to understand why. It has a remarkable ability to survive and reproduce in the most adverse conditions. The first tropical fishes I ever kept as a child were Guppies in an old accumulator jar with no heating but the coal fire and no live food. Nevertheless they lived and bred. They are plentiful and cheap and a good male is one of the most colourful creatures on earth.

In the wild, the female, which is silvery-green, grows to about 2¼ inches, the male, which has small splashes of several metallic colours, to about 1¼ inches. No two males are alike, and there are local variations in the dominant colours. It is this wide palette and variability which makes the Guppy the perfect fish for experimental and

Below: Red Wagtail Platies *Xiphophorus maculatus*
Right: Sailfin Molly *Poecilia latipinna*

selective breeding, and more has been achieved in the way of 'improving' on nature than with any other species. Some fanciers keep nothing but Guppies, and there are national associations striving to codify the latest developments and set appropriate show standards. There are now countless varieties, some classified by the shapes of their tails, some by their colours. Males are now so highly coloured and infinitely varied that an aquarium with many males is a living kaleidoscope.

The possibilities of the male were so great that until very recently the female was completely neglected and remained a dull grey-brown without a hint of colour. Now she has been liberated from her drudgery as wife and mother and come into her own as an exhibition fish.

The Black Molly is one of the best known aquarium fishes. There is no such thing in the wild. All three species, which are found in brackish waters in the states bordering the Gulf of Mexico, are speckled. The Short-finned Molly (*Poecilia sphenops*), from which the Black Molly was developed by patient line-breeding, is a silvery-green with small black flecks. By selecting for more and more black, the Molly we all know – a sooty matt black all over – was produced.

Far more spectacular is the Black Sail-fin Molly, which was produced by crossing a normal Black Molly with a Sailfin Molly (*Poecilia latipinna*) which is yellow with pale blue flecks. The

adult male possesses an enormous flag-like dorsal fin which runs almost the length of his body. It is held erect during the mating display. Another colour variety has recently been achieved, the Golden Sailfin Molly. Its intense orange body speckled with gold brings a blaze of colour to the tank and is a most welcome addition to the live-bearer range.

Most spectacular of all is the Giant Sailfin Molly (*Poecilia velifera*) whose dorsal fin is even larger than the Sailfins. But *P. velifera* is rather large for the aquarium, growing to six inches. Black specimens are very rare, the normal colour being dark orange flecked with pale blue. There is also an attractive smaller molly called the Lyretail which exists in both black and albino forms.

Mollies are extremely tolerant, but to do well they really need slightly salty water with a high pH, plenty of space, and plenty of green food, preferably algae. They will also take lettuce or spinach.

Mollies are easily damaged or shocked by netting and transportation. Moving gravid females will often result in the premature birth of babies which have not digested their yolk sacks or are too heavy to swim. Unlike other live-bearing toothed carps, mollies do not eat their own young.

For the serious breeding of mollies a pair should be given a large well-planted and well-lit tank to themselves and left alone.

The Red Swordtail (*Xiphophorus helleri*) is another famous fish which does not exist in the wild. In Mexico Swordtails are all a drab green. Selective breeding has lengthened the 'sword' (sported only by the male) and produced several handsome colour varieties, but, as always happens with line-breeding, the species has been reduced to about half the size of its wild ancestors, which grow to about five inches, excluding the 'sword'. The 'sword' is not a weapon, merely an extension of the tail.

Swordtails are very easy to keep and breed. When excited, as he usually is, the male shoots backwards and forwards near the female at amazing speed. He is the Casanova of the aquarium, frantically pursuing every female in sight, including those

of other species as well as his own. He is also a great leaper and the glass cover must not be left off with swordtails in the tank.

The first colour varieties were green (with a red line down the length of the body) and red. Both have yellow 'swords' edged with black. Then came the Red-eyed Red, which also has a red 'sword', and the Albino. Now there is the Red Wagtail, with a black tail and sword, the Tuxedo, which sports a black waistcoat as well, the All-black and the Golden. The finnage has also been developed to produce Hi-fins, Lyretails and Veiltails.

The Platy belongs to the same genus as the Swordtail, but is smaller, more chunky and, of course, lacks the 'sword'. The Variegated Platy (*Xiphophorus variatus*) has some colour (the male at least) in the wild, but the Common Platy (*X. maculatus*) from which most of the colour varieties have been developed is a dark bluegreen. Now we have Red, Black, Yellow, Blue and Spangled, and several more elaborate markings such as Sunsets and Bleeding Hearts. Hi-fin varieties have also recently appeared.

Platies are even more hardy than Swordtails and have really no drawbacks at all as a beginner's fish.

FAMILY CYPRINIDAE
Barbs, Danios, Rasboras and Minnows.

This is the largest family of fishes in the world, with about 1,500 species. Almost all have scales but none of the family possess teeth or an adipose fin. This family is found all over the world in tropical and temperate climates with the exception of South America and Australia. The smallest of this family is the *Rasbora maculata*, which is less than one inch, (2.5 cms) and the largest, the Mahseer of India which is over six feet in length. Most species have one or two pairs of barbels, sensitive whiskers which help them to locate worms and other delicacies among the gravel.

The Bitterling has a unique method of reproduction; it is the cuckoo of the fish world, utilizing the freshwater mussel as the keeper of its eggs. The female has a remarkably long ovipositor which she carefully inserts into the mussel and lays a few eggs, the male

Far left: Golden Sailfin Molly *Poecilia latipinna*
Left: Hi-fin Red Swordtail *Xiphophorus helleri*

Far left: Albino Tiger Barbs *Barbus* or
Capoeta tetrazona
Left: *Barbus bimaculatus*
Below: Checker Barb *Barbus* or *Capoeta
oligolepis*

then releases his sperm which is drawn
into the mussel during its process of
filter feeding. The process is repeated,
often for three days until the spawning
is complete. The mussel then looks
after the eggs and the fry until they
become free-swimming.

Most of the other cyprinids are egg
scatterers, and the eggs are non-ad-
hesive. The easiest of the cyprinids to
breed are the Zebra Danio and the
Mountain Minnow. The technique of
spawning is standard for the home
aquarist. The sexes should be separ-
ated for several days and fed on a diet
of live food to bring them into condition. The parent fish, in a ratio of two
males to one female, are introduced at
dusk to a clean aquarium filled to only
two or three inches. The floor of the
aquarium should be covered with
clean pebbles or marbles or a raft of
glass rods bound together so that the
eggs can pass between them but the
fish cannot. The following dawn will
usually bring about spawning. The
females dash around the aquarium
with the males in hot pursuit. The eggs
are scattered wildly and usually sink to
safety, after being fertilized, between
the marbles or rods. The parent fish

should be removed on completion of spawning, but many species would not harm the minute fry, which hatch in two days, were they left in the aquarium with their offspring. One female will usually lay two to three hundred eggs, so the breeding of this type of fish is a good commercial proposition. The fry are usually free-swimming within five to seven days, and should be fed sparingly on a liquid fry food.

Barbs are hardy, active, boisterous fishes, which like plenty of aeration and vegetation. They will live from two to eight years according to size. These fishes are found in rapid, shallow streams throughout tropical Asia and Africa, but not in the New World. They will eat anything and are tolerant of most water conditions, providing the water is clean. Barbs are naturally shoaling fishes and are seen to best advantage in the aquarium in small shoals which will always stick together. The classification of barbs is currently under review, the genus *Barbus* being split into three – *Barbodes*, *Capoeta* and *Puntius*.

The most popular barb has always been the Tiger Barb (*Barbus* or *Capoeta tetrazona*) from Sumatra, with its broad, black, vertical stripes on gold and its

bright red fins. Its main failing is that toothless or not it has a terrible habit of nipping the fins of other fishes. To keep them with any fish which has long flowing fins is to court disaster. The Tiger Barbs are better kept in a shoal where they chase each other and leave the other fishes alone. The females are fuller in the body and the males have a tendency to develop a very red nose when they become excited. There is now also an Albino Tiger Barb. These look very attractive with their pale bodies and pink eyes, but it could be argued that the breeder was striving hard to breed the colour out of an already beautiful fish.

Another popular and hardy little fish is the Rosy Barb (*Barbus* or *Puntius conchonius*) from north-west India. This fish has the colour of beaten silver (with gleaming edges to the large scales), which turns to burnished copper in mating condition. Outside of the breeding season, when his rosy hue has faded, he is still identifiable by the dark tip to his dorsal fin. This is the easiest of the barbs to breed.

A barb which retains his bright colour irrespective of his mating inclinations is the Checker Barb (*Barbus* or *Capoeta oligolepis*) which is found in Sumatra. The scales along the body

Below: Zebra Danio *Brachydanio rerio*
Far right: Giant Danios *Danio malabaricus*

are alternately black and gold, hence the name, but the main feature is the large, black-bordered, orange dorsal fin, which grows darker in the male when mating. They are quite easy to breed in the standard way and the females lay a lot of eggs for their size. They seldom exceed a length of two inches but are very hardy and will survive amazingly low temperatures. Many other barbs are suitable for the beginner and for the community tank, particularly long-standing favourites being the Nigger and Cherry Barbs. A much rarer but very peaceful and attractive barb is *Barbus bimaculatus*.

The danios are a very popular group, presenting no problems to the beginner. The favourite is undoubtedly the small distinctive Zebra Danio (*Brachydanio rerio*) from Bengal, with its blue-black horizontal stripes on silver, always zipping about the tank and practising its quicksilver turns. Equally active and streamlined is the Pearl Danio with its mother-of-pearl shades of pink and mauve which change with the light. The largest of this group is the Giant Danio (*Danio malabaricus*) from the Malabar Coast. They grow to a length of five inches but are still quite peaceful with smaller species. The sexes are almost identical and during spawning they lay adhesive eggs in very large numbers. The parents usually make no attempt to eat the fry, but there is no point in tempting providence, and as the parents do not have a role in the upbringing of their young, they should be removed

Below: Silver Shark *Balanteocheilus melanopterus*
Bottom: Flying Fox *Epalzeorhynchus kallopterous*
Right: Cardinal Tetra *Cheirodon axelrodi*

from the nursery aquarium.

Very similar in shape and habits to the danios are the White Cloud Mountain Minnows (*Tanichthys albonubes*) from Canton, China, where they were first discovered by a Chinese boy-scout called Tan. Baby White Clouds have a neon-like blue light running down the almost transparent body. This fades as they grow, but the adult, which reaches only 1½ inches, remains colourful.

Again with the rasboras there is a clear favourite, the Harlequin (*Rasbora heteromorpha* and *hengeli*) which comes from the Malay Peninsular. The Harlequin has a deeper body than other rasboras. The body colour is a glowing reddish-gold with red fins, but the really distinctive feature is the long,

Another member of the family is the Silver Shark (*Balanteocheilus melanopterus*). Though obviously not a true shark its dorsal fin and general body shape give it that appearance. This species came from Thailand in the early sixties and proved an instant success. It has always been quite expensive but the fish has no bad habits. The Silver Shark is ideally suited for the very large community aquarium. It likes plenty of space. It will grow to a length of fifteen inches and still retain its peaceful character. Another recently discovered fish in this family is the Flying Fox (*Epalzeorhynchus kallopterous*) which has many physical similarities to the pencil fish. This fish is found in Sumatra and is an excellent scavenger. It is also peaceful, even

black triangle in the centre of the rear half. This specimen is a female *R. heteromorpha*. The *R. hengeli* is a smaller fish with a narrower triangle, but is not in my experience paler, as most books claim. Unfortunately it is extremely difficult to breed Harlequins in the aquarium. They are imported in very large numbers.

The most attractive of the other rasboras are the Red Line Rasbora (*R. pauciperforata*) which is like an elongated Glowlight Tetra, and the Redtail Rasbora (*R. steineri*), one of the few fishes to come from the temperate zone of China. All the rasboras prefer soft acid water.

towards the smallest of fishes. It requires a large amount of green food in its diet, so spinach or lettuce must be given if algae is not present.

FAMILY CHARACIDAE
Tetras, Pencil Fishes
and Piranhas

It is one of the largest families in the world – 1,300 species, and new ones are still being discovered. These fishes originate mainly from tropical America with a few from Africa. The major external difference from the cyprinids is that all the characins have an adipose fin and teeth. The great majority of characins are colourful, friendly fishes, undemanding in their diet and perfect for a community aquarium. There are of course exceptions such as the notorious Piranha and the plant eating *Metynnis*. Most of the tetras prefer soft acid water with plenty of cover and soft lighting. The heavy tropical rainfall of the Amazon basin, where many of them are found, continually freshens the streams and pools. Some aquarium water should therefore be replaced with rainwater at frequent intervals.

The breeding habits of this family are similar to most egg scatterers but the eggs are adhesive. They frequently spawn in shoals, but certain members have very interesting characteristics.

The Splash Tetra (*Copeina arnoldi*), although not the most beautiful of fishes has the fascinating breeding technique of leaping out of the water with its mate and depositing its eggs on a leaf above the water line. The parents then spend their time keeping the eggs moist by splashing them, using their well developed tail fins. Glow-light Tetras (*Hemigrammus gracilis* or *erythrozonus*), when mating, will swim alongside each other, lock fins and execute a 'barrel roll' that the most accomplished pilot would admire, scattering their eggs..

Probably the most popular of the characins is the Neon Tetra (*Paracheirodon* or *Hyphessobrycon innesi*) named after W.T. Innes, the author and aquarist, in 1936. This little fish was given international acclaim and is still to this day one of the fastest selling

Below: Lemon Tetras *Hyphessobrycon pulchripinnis*
Far right: Serpae *Hyphessobrycon callistus* or *serpae*

aquarium fishes. In spite of the popularity of this species and years of experience that aquarists have enjoyed, it is still very difficult to breed. The fish will readily accept dry foods, but sifted daphnia is a firm favourite. The Cardinal Tetra (*Cheirodon axelrodi*) was first introduced to the aquatic world in 1956 as a sort of 'Super' Neon Tetra. The deep red underparts run the full length of the body and the fish grows considerably longer. The life expectancy of the Cardinal is also greater than that of the Neon, but it is even more difficult to breed.

One tetra that is relatively easy to

Right: Glowlight Tetra *Hemigrammus gracilis* or *erythrozonus*
Below: Rosy Tetras *Hyphessobrycon rosaceus*
Bottom right: *Hyphessobrycon rubrostigma*

spawn is the Lemon Tetra (*Hyphessobrycon pulchripinnis*). They love to spawn in shoals, but also love to eat their own eggs. It is, therefore, desirable to encourage the spawning to take place in an aquarium densely planted with feathery plants of the Cabomba and Ambulia type; these will provide maximum protection for the adhesive eggs. This is an attractive little fish with a translucent, yellowish body and red eye. The dorsal and anal fins are black, edged with lemon and the Latin name, *pulchripinnis*, means 'pretty fin'. They are quite hardy, very peaceful and grow to a length of 1⅓ inches.

The Rosy Tetra (*Hyphessobrycon rosaceus*) is one of the larger fishes in this family, growing to a length of 2 inches or more. The fish sports a beautiful black flag of a dorsal fin edged in enamel white. The adult male develops a longer dorsal fin and the female has a red tip on the point of hers. A shoal of these fishes is a beautiful sight in any aquarium. They are relatively easy to keep but very difficult to spawn.

The Black Phantom Tetra (*Megalamphodus megalopterus*) is identical to the Rosy Tetra in shape, but smaller and altogether darker. It is also more difficult to breed, and is one of the less common tetras. A more colourful species is the Serpae Tetra (*Hyphessobrycon callistus* or *serpae*), a real jewel of a fish with a bright red anal and tail fin, black dorsal and deep orange body. They were first imported into Europe in 1931 and have grown in popularity ever since. Peaceful yet not afraid of larger species they are far easier to breed than *H. rosaceus*. The male is smaller and slimmer than the female but more brightly coloured.

The Rummy Nosed Tetra (*Hemigrammus rhodostomus*) is longer and slimmer than most tetras. His nose is a vivid red. This colour seems to vary in intensity with the mood of the fish. The species was first introduced into Europe in the early thirties. It is peaceful and highly recommended as a community fish, or, since it will tolerate very acid water and high temperature it is a good fish to keep with Discus. Probably the most attractive of the African species is the Congo Tetra or Congo Salmon (*Micralestes interruptus*) which has metallic rainbow colours and a tail with uneven and rather

ragged extensions of the middle rays.

After considering the other members of the family it is difficult to imagine that the dreaded Piranha (*Serrasalmo nattereri*) could be related to the Neon Tetra. The Piranha's ability to reduce a large animal to a skeleton within a few minutes is not exaggerated. Millions of us have seen it on television. The Piranha has powerful jaws and needle-sharp teeth and an appetite for fresh flesh (including fingers), which is frightening to witness. A rather morbid interest has given this fish a certain popularity as a 'pet', although it can claim a certain beauty with its beaten silver, upper half and rosy, lower body. It is the bulldog jaw that spoils the effect. The usual length of a fully grown specimen is twelve inches (30 cm) and its body is eight inches (20 cm) in depth. It cannot of course be kept with other species.

FAMILY GASTEROPELECIDAE
Hatchets or
Freshwater Flying Fishes
These fish obtain their name from the shape of the body, this great depth of 'chest' accommodating the powerful muscles which enable the fish to fly several yards, skimming above the surface of the water. Unfortunately this is rarely observed by the aquarist. In their natural habitat they feed on small insects, either airborne or surface swimming; in the aquarium they seem to take readily to live daphnia. There are Marbled and Silver species both from the Amazon region. Their colour is not exciting but their shape makes them a very interesting novelty in an aquarium. They are, however, rather delicate and very short-lived, and they have rarely been bred.

FAMILY ANABANTIDAE
Labyrinths
Anabantids have the remarkable ability to 'breathe' in two ways. Not only do they possess conventional gills, they are also equipped with a 'labyrinth' (a cavity in the head), which enables them to absorb oxygen from the air. The labyrinth is a rather complex structure comprising a mass of capillary tubes which bring large surface areas of blood into close proximity with the air. The oxygen is absorbed directly into the blood-stream and waste gases are given off. When the oxygen is exhausted in the labyrinth, the fish surfaces and takes a gulp of fresh air, whilst simultaneously expelling the waste gases through the gills. This auxiliary breathing system enables the fish to be independent of oxygenated water, thereby enabling it to live in a very small volume of water. When male Siamese Fighters (*Betta splendens*) are shipped from Singapore, they are packed in small plastic sachets barely large enough to

Right: Blue Gourami *Trichogaster trichopterus*
Far right: Dwarf Gourami *Colisa lalia*

hold the fishes, with only sufficient water to keep them wet. Amazingly, they will live for days under such conditions. In the mid-sixties male Siamese Fighters in goblets were used as a table decoration in the dining room of a well known New York hotel.

Anabantids are often referred to as 'Bubble Nest Builders'. The male of the species mixes his saliva with air and blows hundreds of tiny bubbles in the form of a raft. This raft is usually anchored and in the case of some of the gouramis is interlaced with plant leaves and algae. The male then displays himself under his nest and awaits a female who is in breeding condition (if he has not been fortunate enough to procure one earlier). The male is often very impatient when a female reveals her willingness to mate. Should the female be rather slow in moving under the nest, he will probably attack her. Should both parties be agreeable, the mating embrace begins. The male wraps his body round the female and they enter a euphoric, trance-like state. As the male squeezes the female, hundreds of eggs fall from her and are instantly fertilized. In the case of gouramis the eggs float upwards into the bubble nest, but the eggs of the Siamese Fighter are heavier than water and sink after fertilization. The male Fighter recovers from the mating before his partner and quickly dives gathering the eggs in his mouth, then blows them into the nest. When spawning is completed, the nest must be constantly repaired and the eggs cared for. In the case of the Fighters this is a task purely for the male and the female is driven away. As the eggs hatch, about two days later, the movement of the fry often breaks the bubbles and the fry fall from the nest. It is the unceasing task of the father for many days to catch or pick up the youngsters and replace them in the nest. When they become free-swimming they follow the father round the aquarium in a dense little shoal and he gently shepherds them. Shortly, however, his paternal instinct may begin to lapse and, if not removed, he will start to eat them.

Gouramis are handsome fishes with a stately manner of swimming, often holding out before them their long pelvic feelers, which were presumably evolved to help them to navigate and identify objects or creatures in very muddy water. By far the handsomest is the Pearl Gourami (*Trichogaster leeri*). This fish originates from the Malay Peninsula and obtains its name from the pearl-like, lacy pattern that covers its body. The male develops a beautiful orange breast, which is very intense during mating. The length of the adult is approximately four inches. Both male and female will care for the young. This species has an unusual appetite for the Hydra, which is a small stinging member of the Coelenterate family and an enemy of most fishes. It is therefore a useful member of a community aquarium.

The Dwarf Gourami (*Colisa lalia*) is as the name suggests, one of the smallest fishes of the gourami family, with a maximum length of approximately $2\frac{1}{2}$ inches. The male is a very colourful and beautiful fish, whilst the female is very drab. They originate from northern India and are accustomed to rather high temperatures, their optimum breeding temperature being 85°F. 29°C. This species is particularly fond of utilizing plants in the bubble nest and both parents will tend the eggs and fry.

The Blue or Three Spot Gourami (*Trichogaster trichopterus*) acquires its second name from the two spots on the body, the third being the eye. They are quite large fish, growing to a length of six inches and can become very aggressive when adult. The male is not very accomplished when it comes to building bubble nests, but this is of no great consequence as both the eggs and the fry float. Like the Pearl Gourami, this species has a taste for the Hydra and occasionally small fishes (including their own young). The males of the Three Spot are of similar coloration to the females, but can be identified by the longer and more pointed dorsal fin.

The Siamese Fighter (*Betta splendens*) was first bred in 1893. Since then it has been developed from a rather dull nondescript creature to a colourful, flamboyant and much sought after aquarium fish in a wide range of colours. The male fighter with his deep rich colours and full flowing fins is always at his best when displaying himself to a female or squaring up to an adversary. The female of the species is relatively insignificant; with dull colouring and small fins but she is quite peaceable and rarely lives up to her name. The male however, has only two reasons for living; fighting and

Left: Siamese Fighters *Betta splendens*

breeding. It is impossible to leave two males together in an aquarium without the certainty that their lovely fins will be tattered rays within minutes.

Most males are peaceful towards any other species, but become enraged by the presence of another male fighter or even by their own reflection in a mirror. In Malaysia large sums are

changes will be beneficial. Earthworms and maggots are good food.

The breeding pattern of this family is worthy of a special mention, and it is a pattern which is closely adhered to by almost every member. Cichlids do not like forced marriages and will sometimes kill the mate carefully chosen by the aquarist.

wagered on fights, staged much as cock-fights were once staged in England. They rarely grow beyond three inches and the rearing of them is a long process. The young take approximately six months to mature and at least eighteen months to reach full size.

FAMILY CICHLIDAE
Cichlids

Cichlids originate in Africa and South America. The family includes some of the largest species kept as aquarium fishes. They are carnivorous and often aggressive and only the dwarf species (which are in any case more beautiful) should be considered for a community tank. Young Angels are almost irresistible and will be good members of a community for many months, but eventually they will reach a size where they can no longer be kept with very small fishes such as Neons. Also many of the larger cichlids habitually pull up plants and make great holes and trenches in the ground. They really need a large tank to themselves with decor mainly in the form of rocks. Heavy filtration and frequent water

If several young fishes are kept together they will pair as they mature. The selection of a partner takes place with what appears to be a wrestling match or trial of strength. The male will lock mouths with a female and 'wrestle' with her for several minutes. Should either partner then retreat, that is usually the end of the romance. If however, the pair continue for several bouts they are likely to become permanent partners. The nesting site selected may be a leaf, a piece of stone, a cave or even a hollow in the gravel, but it is always meticulously cleaned. The cleaning process is carried out by both parents, mouthing and grazing on the site until all traces of algae or dirt have been removed. Often more than one site is prepared. The actual laying of the eggs is often preceded by a further bout of mouth-wrestling before the serious business is commenced. It is at this stage that the female lowers her ovipositor, and the male lowers his sperm tube, which is considerably thinner and more pointed. The female glides slowly over the nesting site, brushing it with her ovipositor and laying a line of adhesive eggs, then she is quickly followed by the male who fertilizes them. Several hundred eggs are laid in this fashion and when the female is emptied of eggs the routine of cleaning begins immediately. The 'mouthing', as the cleansing process is called, takes the form of the parents collecting a few eggs in their mouths, rolling them round, then spitting them back onto the nesting site. Any infertile or ones growing fungus are eaten. The oxygen supply to the eggs is maintained by the parents who create a constantly moving current of water over the nesting site by fanning the water with their pectoral fins. The fanning and mouthing process is maintained until the young become free-swimming. Frequently the parents will decide to 'move house' and take their young with them. This can pre-sent the problem of leaving some of the young unguarded. This is overcome by one of the parents taking a mouthful of young across to the new nesting site, whilst the other also collects a mouthful and stays on guard. As if by some pre-arranged signal, the parents then dash to the opposite site, passing midway, and prepare to perform the reverse process. When the young become free-swimming they will swim in a shoal around their parents who shepherd them about, protecting them from predators.

A typical cichlid in all respects is the Severum or Deacon (*Cichlasoma severum*). It will grow to a length of eight inches and is one of the really aggressive cichlids. This fish has the ability to change colour very rapidly, either to blend in with its background

Left: Siamese Fighter *Betta splendens*
Below: Common Angel *Pterophyllum scalare*

or to express anger. The young of this species look remarkably like the Discus, but as the fish matures it loses its round appearance and the body becomes more elongated. The adult is easily recognizable by the vertical 'dumb-bell' marking in front of the tail. Two handsome smaller cichlids are the Jewel Cichlid (*Hemichromis bimaculatus*) from Africa and the Firemouth (*Cichlasoma meeki*) from S. America, which grow to about 5 in. The former cannot be trusted in a community aquarium, but the Firemouth is usually well-behaved. He has a vivid orange-red throat with loose folds of skin which he blows out when angry.

The best known member of the family is undoubtedly the Angel (*Pterophyllum scalare*) – this common and most graceful fish has a very romantic scientific name – *Pterophyllum* means the winged leaf; and *scalare* refers to the dorsal fin and means, 'like a flight of stairs'. The species originates from the Amazon and Guyana and grows to a length of five inches. The body is extremely compressed, the dorsal and anal fins very long, and the ventral fins even longer so that they look like feelers, though they do not use them as such as the gouramis do. Consequently the Angel is taller than it is long. Its breeding habits follow the cichlid pattern, and the young, when hatched, grow very rapidly. A shoal of baby Angels at an age of five weeks (by which time they have developed to adult shape) following their parents is a wonderful sight. They can easily be frightened during spawning or whilst tending their young, and will eat their brood. Many new varieties have been produced in recent years, including Golden Angels, Half-blacks, Black Veiltails and Marbled Angels.

The dwarf cichlids, especially those of the genus *Apistogramma* are very beautiful and highly coloured and can safely be kept with other small species. But they are delicate fishes which often succumb to disease and which require soft, very clean, and slightly acid water. The apistogrammas are all natives of the Amazon Basin and South America and the largest never exceed three inches. Typical of the genus is Ramirez' Cichlid (*Apistogramma ramirezi*), commonly known as the Ram. This lovely little fish rarely exceeds two inches and has a vivid jewelled body. The male can be easily identified

by the elongated rays at the front of his dorsal fin. A golden variety has been developed which is very beautiful, but it is debatable whether the original Ram can possibly be improved on.

The nearest rival to the Ram among the African dwarf cichlids is the Krib (*Pelmatochromis kribensis*) or (*Pelvicachromis pulcher*), which gets its name from the Kribi River in equatorial west Africa, where it was discovered. This placid fish sports a vivid pink waistcoat, and the smaller female often outshines her male counterpart. When in breeding condition the colours of this fish put it almost on an equal footing with its marine cousins. The Krib is a cave-dweller and prefers to lay its eggs on the roof of a cave-like structure, but once the eggs are

Left: Common and Golden Angels
Pterophyllum scalare
Below: Black Angel *Pterophyllum scalare*
Bottom: Golden Ram *Apistogramma ramirezi*

Right: Krib *Pelmatochromis kribensis*
Bottom right: Firemouth *Chichlosoma meeki*
Far right: Discus *Symphysodom aequifasciata* or *discus*

hatched, they seem to move house two or three times a day. The female spends most of her time looking after the young whilst the male finds and prepares new nesting sites.

The most exotic of all freshwater fishes is the Discus (*Symphysodon aequifasciata* or *discus*), so named because of its shape. This large, showy fish originates from the Amazon and was 'discovered' as an aquarium species in the early thirties. Though basically brown in coloration, the extremities of the fins are often tinged with red and orange and the body is lined with a filigree pattern of azure blue. When Discus are in breeding condition, the intensity of the coloration is considerably increased, the male being brighter. The minimum breeding size is approximately four inches, but adult fishes grow to more than double that size. Discus are fastidious in their feeding habits and seem to prefer a high percentage of live foods of the cyclops, daphnia and fly larvae type. Water for Discus must be extremely clear, soft and acid. It will tolerate an incredibly high temperature. In the wild Discus are frequently trapped in a dry spell in pools where the temperature may reach 110°F. (43°C.). When the rains come and a flush of fresh cool water sweeps into the pools, that is the signal to the Discus to begin spawning.

The newly hatched Discus fry obtain their first food from a mucus or slime which is secreted from the bodies of the parent fish. This 'milk' seems to give all the nourishment required by

the babies until they are fully free-swimming. Discus are prone to a rather odd disease which attacks only this species; it takes the form of deep abscesses about the head and usually proves fatal. Selective breeding has developed many colour strains within this species.

FAMILIES CALLICHTHYIDAE, SCHILBEIDAE AND COBITIDAE
Catfishes and Loaches

These are the cleaners and scavengers of the fish world. They are equipped with whiskers or barbels round their mouths with which they stir up the sand and gravel, and root out any food scraps which may be present. They are primitive fishes which have remained unchanged for millions of years. They are tolerant of worse water conditions than any other family.

The genus *Corydoras* are the smooth armoured catfishes that originate largely from South America. The corydoras usually have two rows of large horny scales running down the length of the body, hence the name 'armoured' catfish. They are relatively peaceful fishes, very hardy and long-lived, ideally suited to aquarium life, and they obtain almost all of their food from the sand or gravel. Most species of the genus have unusually large heads and eyes in relation to the size of their bodies. This gives them an air of innocence which is very endearing.

The corydoras have somewhat unusual breeding habits. After the female has laid her eggs and had them fertilized, she continues to clasp them in her ventral fins until she finds a suitable spot to deposit them. This is usually under a broad leaf which will provide shade for the eggs. On hatching, the young fry are totally self-sufficient and hide in any mulm which is available.

The Leopard Cat (*Corydoras julii*) is a typical example of the smooth armoured cats. It originates from the regions of the Amazon and grows to a length of 2½ inches (7 cm). It is basically silver with black spots like a leopard and a black flag dorsal fin similar to the Serpae Tetra. This species is very peaceable. They spend most of their time hunting for food. Other fishes rarely acknowledge their presence.

Several families are covered by the term catfishes. Some are very different indeed from the corydoras. Many would be considered ugly, or at least an acquired taste. The Pangasius Catfish (*Pangasius sutchi*) belongs to a small family, the Schilbeidae. Most of the species in this family are native to Africa, but Pangasius comes from Thailand.

It swims in a very shark-like manner and, unusually for a catfish, in the middle of the tank. It can be seen from the size of the eye that it is a nocturnal fish. Its food is mainly scavenged from the floor, but it will take any free-swimming insect life. This fish will grow to a length of twelve inches.

Loaches (Cobitidae) have a very wide distribution. They are closely related to the cyprinids but differ from them in never having jaw teeth and possessing three pairs of barbels. Some loaches are like whiskered worms, and only one species, the Clown Loach (*Botia macracantha*), from Sumatra and Borneo, can be described as beautiful. The Clown Loach has two sharp spines in his gill-plate which can be erected when he is handled, to cause his owner a painful jab. He is rather shy, but otherwise an excellent aquarium fish, peaceable and long-lived.

FAMILY MONODACTYLIDAE
Monos and Scats

There are many species of fishes living in the brackish water of estuaries which seem to have the ability to live either in seawater or freshwater. Some of these fishes are very attractive and are kept by both freshwater and marine aquarists. It would seem on balance that the marine aquarist has a greater chance of success with these fishes, as they often contract fin rot and fungus diseases when kept in soft freshwater with a low pH. However, a little aquarium salt added to the freshwater aquarium usually enables the brackish water fishes to feel 'at home'.

Scats (*Scatophagus argus*) are sometimes kept in freshwater aquariums, but they grow very large and are liable to eat the plants. They can be aggressive with smaller fishes at feeding time.

Monos are better fishes for the freshwater tank, especially the Malayan Angel (*Monodactylus argenteus*) from Africa and South East Asia. But even this hardy fish would probably be happier and healthier in brackish or even salt water. Malayan Angels have voracious appetites and quickly grow to a maximum of five inches (12 cm). The silver body reflects the light, and

in a healthy specimen the dorsal fin glows a rich orange. They look particularly effective in a shoal. Neither Monos nor Scats have been bred in captivity.

Top left: *Hemichromis bimaculatus*
Bottom left: Armoured Catfish *Callichthys callichthys*
Above: Clown Loach *Botia macracantha*
Below: Malayan Angel *Monodactylus argenteus*

Marine Tropical Fish in the Home Aquarium

The most beautiful fishes in the world are the aptly-named damsels, butterflies and angels of the coral reefs – damsels dressed in shimmering blue, shot-silk or sequins; butterflies drifting delicately through their underwater garden, as outstanding among fishes as butterflies among insects; angels of a brightness out of this world. The reefs also hold enamelled clowns, fantastically painted wrasses and triggers, pastel-shaded surgeons, and grotesquely beautiful scorpions or dragon-fishes with their gargoyle faces and fairy wings.

The invertebrates of the reef are just as colourful and beautiful. There are some sixty genera of corals with an amazing variety of forms, with shapes like trees and staghorns, fans and lattices, roses and lettuces, mushrooms and brains. The coral we normally see and use as ornaments or to furnish marine aquariums is, of course, merely the white skeleton (except for organ-pipe coral which has a deep red skeleton). Living coral is incredibly colourful and contributes, together with the flower-like anemones and tubeworms, sponges and nudibranchs, to the effect of a magic garden, an underwater paradise. This effect can, to some extent, be recaptured in an invertebrate aquarium. Here we see two Banded Pipefishes (pipefishes are virtually straightened-out sea-horses) swimming through seaweeds, living corals and a variety of invertebrates.

And a paradise it is for thousands of other creatures. The reef affords a multiplicity of habitats – the living coral heads themselves, piles of coral debris, rocks, caves, sand, meadows of algae. Here thrive the molluscs: oysters, mussels, clams, scallops, snails, octopuses and squids; the spiny echinoderms: sea-urchins and star-fishes; the many-legged arthropods: crabs, lobsters and shrimps.

And so, for the small fishes, the reef affords both protection and abundant food. Predators are few, pickings are rich, and life is good for these pampered beauties.

All the rich life of the reef depends upon the humble coral polyp. The coral polyp is part animal, part plant, since part of its body tissue is composed of algae. This algae, like all plants, needs sunlight, so coral does not grow at a depth of much more than about 130 feet, and

View of corals, etc, with left: juvenile Koran Angel *Pomacanthus semicirculatus*, and right: Royal Gramma *Gramma loreto*.

the lushest growth is down to about sixty feet on the seaward precipice of the reef, where there is also plenty of oxygen and plankton.

The coral polyp is like a miniature anemone. It feeds by filtering plankton from the water. It also extracts from the water calcium carbonate with which it builds, upon the skeletons of its ancestors, its own external skeleton. An individual coral head can grow up to ten inches in a year, and a reef can grow at a rate of six feet a year. At the same time, of course, the reef is being broken down under the stress of storms, or the attentions of the parrot-fish with its coral-crunching teeth and cement-mixer stomach, or the crown-of-thorns starfish fast demolishing the Great Barrier Reef. Now there is the additional threat of the hatchet-happy tourist. Pollution is also killing many reefs. The problem is so bad that it is quite possible that the living reefs, where the helmet-crab has lived unchanged for 400 million years, will no longer be there for our grandchildren to see.

A single reef can support up to 400 species of fishes. Each has its ecological niche, both in terms of territory and of food supply. One species will hide in a coral head, another among the debris, another in a cave or crevice, another in a shell, another among weeds or among the tentacles of an anemone, and yet another will burrow in the sand. One species will feed mainly on coral, another on small crustaceans, another on molluscs, another on echinoderms, another on algae, another on smaller fishes . . . Thus the need, in a community aquarium, to offer a widely varied diet.

Some fishes habitually move about in shoals, sometimes comprising thousands of individuals. Some patrol a strictly limited territory singly or in pairs. Schooling, the tendency of some fishes to get as close to each other as possible at moments of danger, seems to work by confusing the predator, who cannot focus on or concentrate on any specific victim. Sometimes the school becomes a mob, effectively driving off a large invader by sheer weight of numbers.

The typical muscular streamlined shape of the fast-swimming fishes of the open sea, of which the shark, if we could see it without fear, is the most beautiful, is not found in coral fishes. They are specialized not for sustained speed, but for acceleration over short distances and manoeuvrability. A large school of damsels can, in a twinkling, completely disappear into a small coral head. The disc-shaped butterfly quickly slides into a narrow crevice where no predator can follow.

Though the shapes of the reef fishes can be seen to be functional, it is more difficult to see their patterns and colours as anything but the extravagance of nature delighting in variety and vividness and beauty, splashing

her paints exuberantly here, subtly shading and delicately cross-hatching there. A few species are obviously camouflaged, or have patterns which, like the stripes and patches of jungle animals, break up the outline. But in the majority of species there can be no question of camouflage. On the contrary, they are advertising their presence to the world, but especially to other members of the same species. Thus the utter distinctiveness of each species eliminates the danger both of overcrowding that particular niche, and of sterile cross-mating. The more different species of the same family there are in the vicinity, the more startling the variations of pattern and colour, which will have evolved to help them recognize their own species at a distance in the blue undersea dusk. When we expose these colours to ideal lighting in the aquarium, the result is breathtaking.

Marine Tropical Fishes in the Home Aquarium

Marine tropicals are very much more difficult to keep in the home aquarium than freshwater tropicals, not because they are less hardy (they are, in fact, hardier) but because it is so much more difficult to create in the home aquarium

Left: *Amphiprion perideraion*
Below: Cowrie and Flame Scallop
Right: Mantis Shrimp

anything resembling the conditions in the reef than it is to duplicate the natural conditions of freshwater fishes. Until a few years ago the chance of keeping a butterfly or an angel alive for a year was negligible. There have been major improvements in shipping, disease control, feeding, and the artificial seawater preparations, but the crucial breakthrough has been in filtration. The undergravel bacteriological filtration system now generally in use has solved the problem of the gradual build up of nitrites highly toxic to these fishes. The system is essentially the same as that used in the gravel beds at sewage works. When an aquarium has been in use for a few weeks each piece of gravel becomes coated with bacteria. Simple air-lifts pull the water down through the gravel into a chamber beneath it, then up pipes and back into the tank from just above the surface (thus aerating the water at the same time). As molecules of nitrite pass through the gravel the aerobic bacteria add oxygen, thus converting toxic nitrite into harmless nitrate. The system has the further advantage of being cheap and easy to construct with little to go wrong if the pump is kept working. An efficient pump will circulate the entire contents of the aquarium in fifteen minutes. Some aquarists advocate external power filters with activated carbon, ozonizers, protein-skimmers, etc. in addition, but they are not strictly necessary.

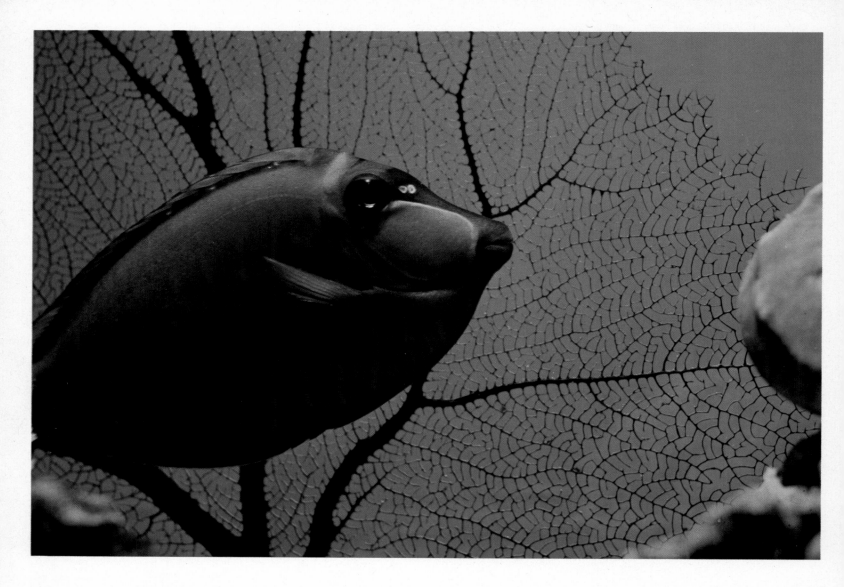

Above: Unicorn Tang *Naso lituratus*
Right: Seahorse *Hippocampus kuda*

One of the principle difficulties in keeping a community of freshwater fishes is, as we have seen, the very different requirements of different species in terms of temperature, pH, hardness etc. Though it may be more difficult to duplicate the water conditions of a coral reef, at least there is the advantage with marines that once you have got it right, you know that it is right for all species, since there is little difference between one coral reef and another the world over. On the other hand there are so many delicate or impossible marine fishes and so many with special requirements that the aquarist who simply buys what catches his eye at the shop must anticipate high losses, even if the conditions in his tank are right. But, by restricting himself to those species agreed to be hardy (and this is no very crippling restriction) his losses need be no greater than he would expect with freshwater fishes. If the environment stays right and a fish settles in, eats well, and survives those crucial first weeks, there is no reason why it should not live happily for years.

The marine aquarist needs money, time and knowledge. There is no space here to go into all the complexities and no reader should attempt to set up a marine tank solely on the information I am able to give, but here are a few of the essentials.

The tank should be as large as possible, preferably fifty to a hundred gallons, certainly not less than twenty gallons. An all-glass or fibre-glass tank is best. If the tank has a metal frame it must be nylon-coated before glazing. Any metal in contact with the water will rapidly poison the fish. Salt water dissolves putty, so the inside of the tank must be sealed with silicone-rubber.

Plants will grow in the aquarium only if special steps are taken to provide high light intensity (in the form of spotlights) and vitamin additives, but the tank can be decorated with coral skeletons and shells. These must be cleaned, boiled and bleached very carefully to remove all traces of organic matter (and rinsed many times to remove all traces of bleach). I always try to make my own tanks look as much like a section of a coral reef as I can. This means arranging the coral to look as if it were growing from the rock, not just piling one piece on another, or arranging the pieces like ornaments on a shelf. And no plastic divers or sunken galleons!

Those who live far from the habitats of these fish should use a reputable brand of prepared salts to make artificial sea water. The specific gravity at 75°F should be 1.020 to 1.022. Trace elements should be added occasionally. It is wise to change a quarter of the water every few months, also to remove the sea-humus which accumulates in the gravel. Every marine aquarist needs a hydrometer, a nitrite test kit and a pH test kit. The pH should be 8.0 to 8.3. To maintain this high pH layers of crushed limestone, crushed cockle shell and coral sand should be used instead of gravel, and rockwork should be limestone or tufa. A few drops of buffer solution weekly may also be necessary.

The temperature of the water must be thermostatically controlled at about 76°F. (25°C.). The tank should be well lit with, ideally, both fluorescent and tungsten lighting, and the lights should be on the length of a tropical day. This encourages the growth of beneficial green algae.

No fishes should be put in the aquarium until all the systems and readings have been perfect for a week or two, then only two or three hardy damsels should be introduced and fed sparingly until the bacteria culture has had time to develop, and that may take several weeks. The hardiest, most nitrite resistant fish are the Humbug and Domino Damsels. Also very hardy are the other damsels, the Cleaner and Lyretail Wrasses, scorpions and triggers. Clowns are relatively sensitive and not suitable for absolute beginners.

The tank must not be overcrowded. One inch of fish to every two gallons should be an absolute limit. The beginner would be wise to limit himself to one every four gallons for a few months.

Most of the fishes offered for sale are babies. Some of them, especially scorpions, batfishes and triggers, will grow very fast and will need more and more room. This

should be allowed for in stocking the tank, unless an arrangement can be made with a dealer for trading in the big fellows. There is a demand for them from the public aquariums and from fanciers with enormous tanks.

When buying fishes, first choose your dealer. Does he seem to know what he is talking about? Is the water in his tanks clear and are the fishes active and healthy and eating. Examine a fish carefully for wounds, fungus, marks or blotches of any kind which might indicate disease. If it is marked in any way, if it is lying on the bottom or gulping at the surface or breathing very fast or listless or persistently rubbing itself or pale, if its fins are permanently closed or fully extended, don't buy it. If the dealer says it is eating, ask him to show you. If, on the other hand, a fish is immaculate in body and fins, swimming about bright-eyed and alert, in good colour, breathing normally, eating, and frequently closing or extending its fins, don't quibble if you are asked a little more for it than you had intended to pay. A cheap but sick fish may not only die, but may introduce disease into your tank and kill them all.

There are a few exceptions to this rule. Some wrasses normally lie on the bottom; batfishes stay near the surface; scorpions stay still for long periods, often hanging upside-down; and many perfectly fit fishes may hide out of normal shyness, especially if it is only a few days since

Below: General shot of tank with Scorpion and Domino Damsel
Right: Blue-faced Angel *Euxiphipops xanthometapon*

they were in their familiar reef.

The dealer is, to some extent, at the mercy of the collectors. In the Philippines, for example, where many of the finest fishes come from, all the collecting is done by daylight (owing to local superstitions among the fishermen) and the commonest method is to knock out the fishes by squirting sodium cyanide in their faces. Needless to say, these fishes are still groggy when they arrive in the shops and there are high losses. In the Caribbean, the standard method is the use of baited traps, but this results in a large number of injuries. By far the best method is that generally used in Sri Lanka, where the collecting is done at night with underwater torches. The fishes are asleep and can be picked up by hand.

If you have a long way to go, your fishes should be in large plastic bags with plenty of oxygen, each inside another plastic bag, inside a polystyrene-lined box packed with paper and sealed. They are shipped from the tropics like this, and will usually survive for up to forty-eight hours. When you get them home, do not suddenly expose them to light or to any other sudden change. Float the plastic bag in your tank for half-an-hour, occasionally adding half a cupful of water from the tank. Thus both temperature and water-chemistry are gradually equalized.

Most of the fishes commonly sold will live happily with other species, but many will not tolerate other members of their own. Once established, a fish will come to regard part of the tank, or even the whole tank, as its own preserve, and will resent (often violently) the introduction of new fishes. It is therefore a good plan to put a new fish behind a removable glass partition at one end of the tank, or in a perforated clear plastic box for a few days until the established fishes have come to accept its presence. Angels and surgeons are particularly territorial and it is wise to settle for one of each in a tank. This does not apply to schooling genera such as *Dascyllus*, *Chromis*, *Amphyprion* and *Apogon*, though adults of these genera will become aggressive when they pair. Every tank should have a Cleaner Wrasse (*Labroides dimidiatus*) which will remove parasites from the other fishes and clean their wounds.

Marine tropical fishes are susceptible to several kinds of parasitic and fungus diseases. There are reliable chemical treatments available, or an ozonizer is an effective prophylactic and sterilizer. It is imperative that no treatment should be used which destroys the bacteria indispensable to the filtration system. Most of the chemical treatments are fatal to invertebrates.

Since many marine fishes in the reefs eat mainly food which cannot be provided in the home aquarium – the larger plankton, coral polyps, small crustaceans, marine algae – they have to be educated to eat what can be provided and success or failure in this is obviously a matter of life and death. Some species, especially some of the most beautiful butterflies are impossible or so difficult that they should not be imported, but most of the fishes offered to aquarists can be tempted. The secret is variety. Feed the fishes as much as they will consume as you watch; feed often, and try everything. Even when your fishes are all eating well you will still have to maintain this variety, as they will all have different likes and dislikes. Here are some of the basic foods: live mussels, (chopped and sterilized by pouring boiling water over them), squid, adult brine shrimps or frozen mysis, daphnia, glassworm,

bloodworm, tubifex, earthworm (chopped and washed), whiteworm; any shellfish; scraped raw fish or meat; freeze-dried brine shrimps; chopped spinach or lettuce; various proprietary flaked and granulated foods.

Damsels and clowns will spawn freely and the eggs will hatch, and there are reports of people in various parts of the world raising the young to adulthood. But there is no method generally available to amateur aquarists to feed the fry, which will die in a few days without live plankton. Baby seahorses and scorpions have reputedly been raised on newly-hatched brine shrimps.

The exact identification of species of marine tropicals may cause problems. A great deal of reclassification is now in progress. The old classification was very bad, consigning some fishes to the wrong family altogether, and classifying others as different species, which are now known to be only colour-phases of the same species. There are also wide variations between individuals in some species (Sea Bee Clowns for example) which have led to a multiplicity of unnecessary distinctions in classification.

The classification used in this book is based on *Pacific Marine Fishes* by Burgess and Axelrod, or, for species not covered by that work, on *Exotic Marine Fishes* by Axelrod and Emmens. Some very recent reclassifications have not yet passed into general use, so that fishes will often be offered for sale under obsolete scientific names. I have therefore also indicated some of the commonest of these.

The Fishes

FAMILY POMACENTRIDAE
Damsels

Damsels are hardy and cheap and of great character. Some species are hardly to be beaten for beauty by fishes at any price. The beginner would be well-advised to start with damsels, particularly of the genus *Dascyllus*: the Humbug Damsel (*D. aruanus*), the Domino or Three-spot Damsel (*D. trimaculatus*) or the Cloudy Damsel (*D. carneus*). The Atlantic Domino Damsel (*D. albisella*) differs from the Indo-Pacific Domino in having larger and more elongated white spots. In both species the spots reduce with age until they disappear altogether. The Pacific Cloudy Damsel (*D. reticulatus*) is a duller fish than its counterpart *D. carneus*, which is found in the Indian Ocean and the Red Sea. Black, white and grey are the predominant colours in *Dascyllus*, and they prove that bright colours are not necessary for attractiveness. They are resistant to disease, low pH and the high nitrite level which is inevitable in the first weeks after a new tank has been set up. They will, like all the damsels, eat almost anything.

Although they will not grow to much more than two inches in captivity, damsels are very territorial and aggressive and quite capable of buffeting to death a much larger fish which has no means of escape in a small tank. *Dascyllus*, especially the Domino Damsel, puts his head down and charges like a little bull. He will also charge the hand that feeds him, and his aggression call, a loud grunting, can be heard at the other end of the room. Damsels will attack other members of their own species with particular savagery. They should be bought singly or in groups of ten or more. With a large number the schooling instinct seems to override the territorial instinct. In the reef a school of damsels will mob even an octopus or a barracuda.

Damsels should be provided with large coral heads. They will dart through the narrow convolutions of the coral with incredible agility, sometimes even swimming backwards, and are so attached to their coral refuge that they will remain in it even when it is lifted out of the water. Many a piece of coral has been taken to the sink to wash with a Cleaner Wrasse and half a dozen damsels completely concealed within it.

The Domino Damsel has the ability, unique among damsels, to enter the tentacles of even the most poisonous

Left: Yellow Tang *Zebrasoma flavescens*
Above: Yellow-tailed Blue Damsel *Abudefduf parasema*

anemones (including those from the Mediterranean where there are no damsels) with impunity. Presumably the purpose of this and the manner in which it is achieved are much the same as in the case of clowns, which are also known as anemone fishes for this reason.

Several damsels can change colour radically as a result of fright or changes of light. An Electric Blue Damsel (*Abudefduf uniocellata*, formerly *Pomacentrus caeruleus*) which lives up to its name in the dealer's tank, may be almost black in its plastic bag. Don't tell the poor man he has brought the wrong fish! The Green Damsel (*Chromis caeruleus*) is similar in that it is constantly changing from green to blue as the light catches it.

Some damsels such as the Yellowtail Blue (*Abudefduf parasema* formerly *Pomacentrus melanochir*) and the Thai Damsel, excavate caverns for themselves by carrying the larger pieces of debris away in their mouths and wafting the smaller ones away by rapidly vibrating their tails. Another lovely damsel, but rarely imported is the Fijian Blue Damsel.

Damsels will often spawn in the aquarium. The male, who becomes even more aggressive than usual, lures the female, or several females, to his chosen spot where the eggs are deposited. Then he drives off the female, guards the eggs, and oxygenates them by fanning them with his tail until they hatch. The babies are then on their own.

Clowns or Anemonefishes

Clowns are not as suitable as damsels for the beginner because they are less tolerant of nitrite and generally less hardy. But, if conditions are right, they are excellent aquarium fishes, particularly the Common Clowns (*Amphiprion ocellaris* or *percula*) which are cheap and easily available, omnivorous, sociable, entertaining, and very gaily coloured with their distinctive bands of bright orange and enamel white. *A. percula* has a thicker black border to its white bands than *A. ocellaris*. Nearly all the clowns have these white bands on a background of red, orange, pink, maroon or brown. Other species, such as the Tomato or Fire Clown (*A. frenatus*, previously

Above: Sea Bee *Amphiprion clarkii*
Below: Humbug Damsel *Dascyllus aruanus*
Right: Common Clowns *Amphiprion ocellaris* or *percula*

ephippium), the Sea Bee (*A. clarkii*, previously *sebae* and *xanthurus*) or the Maroon Clown (*A. biaculeatus*) are less sociable and should not be mixed. (The Maroon Clown differs from all other *Amphiprion* species in having gill-plate spikes like those of angels. For this reason it was until recently allocated to a different genus, *Premnas*.) The Pink Clown (*A. perideraion*) is a schooling fish and should not be kept without anemones. Clowns are found throughout the tropical Indo-Pacific, but not in the Atlantic.

The changed scientific names of so many species (not only of clowns) are the result of recent reclassification in the light of evidence that fishes formerly thought to be of different species because of their quite distinct markings are in fact colour phases of the same species. The Tomato Clown, for example, is bright orange-red as a juvenile, except for his white head-stripe but as he grows the middle of his body becomes darker, eventually almost black. The background colour of the juvenile Sea Bee is bright orange-yellow, but in the adult it is uniformly brown.

Clowns differ from damsels not only in coloration but in their whole lifestyle, which centres on their symbiosis or partnership with anemones. The flower-like anemone gently waves its tentacles in the current. But each tentacle is loaded with stinging cells (nematocysts), little hypodermics triggered at a touch to inject a paralysing poison into the victim. Only the clown is immune. Not only does he survive contact with the anemone, he even seeks it, nestling in the very mouth of the anemone, and rubbing himself constantly and with evident enjoyment among the lethal tentacles.

This relationship was first observed over a century ago, but it has only recently been explained. If the anemone's stinging mechanism were triggered by any kind of touch, it would constantly be stinging itself and its neighbouring anemones. To prevent this, anemones secrete a mucus which inhibits the stinging mechanism. The clown has cracked this secret. He has found that by tentatively rubbing himself against the non-stinging parts of the anemone or by enduring for a while the light stings as he gingerly flicks against a tentacle, he can gradually coat himself with this protective mucus and become as safe as if he were

part of the anemone. When the mucus is removed experimentally, *Amphiprion* is stung like any other fish until he has had time to repeat the process of acclimation.

The anemone becomes home for the clown, which chases off the anemone's enemies (several butterflies, for example, will nibble at the tentacles) with a ferocity amazing in so small a fish. Even human divers will be attacked by breeding clowns, and if the going gets too rough the clown can always retreat to the protection of the anemone.

Compared with the damsel, the clown is sluggish in his movements, not venturing far from his anemone and not needing the manoeuvrability the damsels have evolved to swim in and out of coral heads. His bright and distinctive coloration is also probably related to his symbiosis with the anemone. If a predator comes too near and is stung, he comes to associate the clown's colours with getting stung and may thereafter give him a wide berth even when the clown is away from his anemone refuge.

In the aquarium a clown will feed his host anemone by dropping into it any pieces of food too big for him to swallow. It is not known whether this also happens in the reef, but seems likely. If a clown has no anemone to feed in the aquarium, he will often choose an anemone-substitute in the form of a conch or other hollow shell, and assiduously 'feed' it with large morsels. Unless some other fish or invertebrate regularly cleans out this larder, there could soon be pollution from the rotting mass.

The anemone also offers protection for the eggs of *Amphiprion* which are usually laid in its shadow on a smooth patch of rock which the clown has carefully cleaned. All the Pomacentridae anchor their eggs firmly. *Amphiprion* may lay several hundred cylindrical eggs, each about an eighth of an inch long. The male watches over them for about ten days constantly fanning them with his fins. Many, nevertheless, are eaten by crabs, and many are infertile. The remainder hatch and become part of the plankton which is the main food supply of the parents. The process is repeated several times at intervals of ten days.

To spawn clowns in captivity a healthy adult pair should be given a tank to themselves with a few large anemones and adjacent smooth rocks.

Left: Tomato Clown *Amphiprion frenatus*
Above: Maroon Clown *Amphiprion biaculeatus* with Yellow-tailed Blue Damsels *Abudefduf parasema*

They seem to prefer a lower pH than other marines – perhaps even slightly acid. The eggs will hatch in about six days, but the young will quickly die without live plankton.

FAMILY LABRIDAE
Wrasses

The family of wrasses covers a great range of species, from the diminutive genus *Labroides*, seldom exceeding three inches, to the giants of the genus *Cheilinus* several feet long. Most of the smaller imported species live on small invertebrates, which they crush with their strong protruding teeth; but they rarely trouble other fishes in the aquarium.

Many species are extremely colourful. The Clown Wrasse (*Coris gaimard*) is trebly so, since he passes through three quite different but equally gaudy colour phases. The juvenile is vivid orange with five, large, black-edged, white spots or saddles along his back. These soon disappear, the tail becomes yellow, the body-colour darkens, particularly the rear half which becomes spangled with bright blue dots. The fish undergoes another complete transformation before it becomes an adult.

The wrasses have a strangely laboured method of swimming, with the pectorals used like oars, jerking their length along. But this applies only to cruising. When a wrasse wants to move, he can move. Drop a mussel in the opposite end of the tank and he will streak across to snatch it from under the noses of the nearer fishes. Some wrasses, the Lyretail (*Thalassoma lunare*) for example, like to lie on the bottom, often resting their chin on a shell. Others, such as the Clown Wrasse or Green Wrasse (*Halichoeres melanurus*) spend the night under the gravel and will do a spectacular nose-dive into it if frightened.

In the reef the wrasses have a unique mating procedure. A large group will mill around excitedly near the bottom. Several will suddenly break away, dash to the surface, then abruptly turn back, releasing at that moment a cloud of eggs and sperm. The turbulence created ensures that most of the eggs are fertilized. The eggs immediately float to the surface.

Wrasses are very susceptible to shock and consequently do not travel well. A wrasse in a state of shock should be left in darkness until the natural light of dawn slowly infiltrates the tank. Once settled in they present no problems.

One of the most fascinating sights to be seen in the aquarium is that of a tiny silver and pale-blue fish with a black central stripe swimming between the deadly spines, in and out of the gills, or even in and out of the mouth of a large scorpionfish, which would swallow in one gulp any other fish of that size. Or sometimes you will see a queue of larger fishes waiting their turn and when it comes, presenting themselves to the attentions of this intrepid little fellow. For he is the Cleaner Wrasse (*Labroides dimidiatus*), the barber and general practitioner of the reef, who removes the parasites from the skin, mouths and gills of all the other fishes and cleans their wounds. With the help of the cleaner shrimps, which also have their recognized surgeries or cleaning-stations, he keeps the other fishes healthy and comfortable, and in return they give him safe conduct wherever he goes.

The cleaning operation must be of tremendous importance to override such primary instincts as the predatory instinct of the clients and the fear of the cleaners. Moreover, a general truce seems to hold for the whole cleaning station area, where fishes will patiently queue next to fishes they would be in mortal fear of anywhere else. Even sharks will come in from the open sea for cleaning and abide by the general truce. When a population of Cleaner Wrasses was removed experimentally from a crowded reef, the reef was abandoned within two weeks. When the wrasses were replaced, the others rapidly returned.

Apparently, the Cleaner is recognized as such by his uniform, for the Neon Goby, which performs the same function wears the same uniform. And so, with fiendish cunning, does the Saw-tooth Blenny (*Aspidontus taeniatus*) who is not a cleaner but a confidence trickster, for he exploits the immunity his uniform brings him to get in close only to take a chunk out of his unsuspecting host before beating a hasty retreat.

In the reef the Cleaner Wrasse may get his entire food supply from his cleaning operations, but in the aquarium he will eat almost anything. No tank should be without its Cleaner Wrasse. Perhaps it would be kinder to have two, or who cleans the Cleaner? I have kept two together for a short

Far left above: Clown Wrasse *Coris gaimard*
Far left below: Green Wrasse *Halichoeres melanurus*
Left: Lyretail Wrasse *Thalassoma lunare*

time, but never observed them cleaning each other. Cleaner Wrasses are very susceptible to nitrite and to immature synthetic sea-water and should not be introduced to a new aquarium for at least two months.

The strangest of the wrasses in appearance is the Bird-mouth Wrasse (*Gomphosus varius*, formerly *coeruleus*), whose mouth is elongated into the shape of a duck-bill. The male is a deep blue-green, the female predominantly brown. *Gomphosus* is an active, hardy and entertaining aquarium fish.

FAMILY CHAETODONTIDAE
Butterflies

There are over two hundred species of butterflies. The greatest concentration is around the islands of Indonesia where there are over sixty species. But they are found in every coral reef. Butterflies are very territorial, and a single pair may lay claim (as far as their own species is concerned) to a stretch of reef a quarter of a mile long. Thus, if the particular ecological niche filled by butterflies is to be fully exploited, it can only be by a proliferation of species, much to the delight of the natural historian, aquarist and photographer.

Most species have a wide distribution throughout the Indo-Pacific, but some are more localized. *Chaetodon collaris* and *C. xanthocephalus* are found only in the Indian Ocean, *C. larvatus*, *C. semilarvatus*, *C. fasciatus* and *C. mesoleucus* only in the Red Sea, *C. capistratus*, *C. ocellatus* and *C. striatus* only in the Atlantic. Fishes from the Red Sea are happier at a rather higher temperature (80–85°F.) and salinity (at least 1.025) than those from anywhere else.

All the butterflies are basically disc-shaped and so laterally compressed that a four-inch fish can swim with ease through a half-inch gap. In the sea the smallest species grow to about four inches, the largest to about twelve, but in the aquarium growth is inhibited, and a specimen acquired at two or three inches will seldom grow to more than four.

Butterflies are not as spectacular as angels, but more subtle and delicate in their patterns and coloration. Several species have an attractive reticulated pattern, each scale outlined in a darker colour. This is most clearly seen in the Pakistani Butterfly (*C. collaris*), *C. rafflesi* and *C. xanthurus*. Two other species show an interesting chevron pattern – *C. triangulum* and *C. mertensi*.

One of the most striking butterflies is the Saddleback (*C. ephippium*), found only in the Pacific. The juvenile is about four inches long. As he matures he will lose his eyestripe and gain a long filament at the back of his dorsal fin. *C. auriga* has a similar filament.

The Bannerfish (*Heniochus acuminatus*) differs from all other butterflies in having an extremely elongated fourth dorsal spine, often longer than the body, carrying a white fin like a banner. *H. acuminatus* is probably the hardiest of all the butterflies. They survive the pollution of Colombo harbour, and I have know them none the worse after twenty-four hours in cold water. Another characteristic of the genus *Heniochus* is the development in mature specimens of horns on the forehead in several species but not in *H. acuminatus*. The Bannerfish also differs from other butterflies (except *C. semilarvatus*) in its schooling habit. All others pair for life.

The Moorish Idol (*Zanclus canascens*) is not strictly a butterfly, but has a family all to itself, the Zanclidae. It is similar to the Bannerfish, though completely unrelated and much more exotic. Some call the Bannerfish 'the poor man's Moorish Idol'. The Moorish Idol is one of those fishes which, like the seahorse or scorpion, seems to belong more to the world of fantasy than that of nature. Small groups of Moorish Idols move about the reef, peacefully browsing on invertebrates and algae. They eat ravenously in captivity, but nevertheless commonly die in a very short time.

Apart from their markings, butterflies differ from angels in being slimmer, in lacking the cheek-spine, and in the fact that the young pass through a larval stage, called the *tholichthys*, during which the head is covered with bony plates which gradually disappear as they approach the juvenile stage.

Above top: Butterfly *Chaetodon mesoleucus*
Above: Butterfly *Chaetodon rafflesi*
Right: Butterfly *Chaetodon mertensi*
Opposite page top: Pakistani Butterfly *Chaetodon collaris*
Opposite page bottom: Addis Butterfly *Chaetodon semilarvatus* with Cleaner Wrasse *Labroides dimidiatus*

Again unlike angels, there is little significant difference in markings between juveniles and adults. Thus, the juveniles would be attacked and driven off if they approached the territory of the adults, and must find different feeding grounds often in the tidal pools.

It is common for butterflies to have an ocellus, or false eye, somewhere on the fins or body towards the rear. Usually the real eye is disguised by a stripe running through it, or, in the case of the Long-nose (*Forcipiger flavissimus* or *longirostris*) by a black mask which makes him look like a rather sinister highwayman. The combination of realistic false eye and well-disguised real eye is particularly evident in the Copperband (*Chelmon*

Far left: Copperband Butterfly *Chelmon rostratus*
Left: Rainbow Butterfly *Chaetodon trifasciatus* with Bannerfishes *Heniochus acuminatus*
Below: Saddleback Butterfly *Chaetodon ephippium*
Bottom: Long-nosed Butterfly *Forcipiger longirostris*

rostratus). Apparently the aggressor normally aims at the eye. If he aims at the wrong one, he gets a mouthful of water, for his intended victim has gone the other way. Copperbands even fool one another. When fighting they can be seen to be concentrating their attack on the false eye, thus doing much less damage than if they were to attack the real one. The very small mouths of these two species make it essential to give them such foods as mussel and earthworm finely chopped.

Butterflies have relatively small mouths, with several rows of close slender teeth, like a brush. Hence the name chaetodonts which means 'bristle-teeth'. They eat the larger plankton, small crustaceans and coral polyps. Those with long snouts such as the Long-nose and Copperband are obviously specialized for picking or sucking out small crustaceans from crevices in the rocks, and corals. Those without snouts such as *C. trifasciatus*, *C. meyeri*, *C. ornatissimus*, *C. plebius*, *C. larvatus*, *C. octofasciatus*, and *C. trifascialis* probably feed almost exclusively on coral polyps, and are therefore extremely difficult to feed in the aquarium. Unfortunately, these are some of the loveliest species, and aquarists find them irresistible. But the temptation should be resisted to discourage their importation. A good rule of thumb for the aquarist buying butterflies is – the shorter the snout the harder to feed. An exception is *C. triangulum*, which has a snout, but will not eat.

The easiest butterflies are the Long-nose and Copperband, the Bannerfish, *C. auriga*, *C. lunula*, *C. vagabundus*, *C. pictus*, *C. ephippium*, *C. rafflesi*, *C. semilarvatus*, *C. falcula*, *C. mertensi*. The very distinctive and attractive Pakistani Butterfly (*C. collaris*) may be reluctant to start feeding, but once started will eat anything and is as tough as they come.

To say that these are the easiest butterflies is not to say that they are easy. Few butterflies will stand a low pH or the slightest trace of nitrite. A great variety of food, including fresh and live food, must be offered. The Long-nose and Copperband cannot manage large chunks, so their favourite foods, mussel and earthworm, must be finely chopped. On the other hand, it need not be assumed that butterflies will eat only fresh and live food. Most love freeze-dried brine shrimp, and many will eat flakes.

A newly-acquired butterfly which is not eating may often be tempted by small earthworms chopped into half-inch lengths, by mussel offered in the half shell, or by pieces of mussel rubbed onto the coral where the fish has been vainly pecking. A temporary lowering of the specific gravity to 1.8 or 1.9 often has the effect of stimulating appetite.

Apart from Bannerfishes and *C. semilarvatus*, which are schooling fishes, butterflies should be kept apart from their own species. An established butterfly will probably resent the introduction of a new butterfly of any species to his tank. The first six or seven dorsal spines on a butterfly are

pouring medicaments into the tank; when the light has been on for a few minutes he will be swimming normally again.

FAMILY POMACANTHIDAE
Angels

The angels are the most resplendent of all the reef fishes, the aristocrats of the reef as their common names imply – Regal, Majestic, Queen, Emperor. They are expensive because they need to be shipped singly with a good deal of water, so that, as with other large fishes, only 20% of the cost to the dealer is the price of the fish; the other 80% is what it costs him for transportation. Fortunately, though shy, they are less delicate than many butterflies in the home aquarium.

long, sharp and erectile. Fortunately, they are used mainly for defence. They attack with the snout and by general buffeting, seldom killing each other. But the loser (which is always the new fish, even when he is the larger) may be so bruised and frightened that he skulks in a corner and soon starves to death. You may be lucky and have no trouble, but there is nothing lost by having a perforated plastic box ready just in case.

A note of warning, finally, to owners of Long-nosed Butterflies. This fish has thrown many an aquarist into a needless panic by its habit of sleeping upside-down. There is no need to start

They are disc-shaped, like the butterflies, but not so slender, and, except for the dwarf angels, are considerably larger. Some species grow to two feet in the sea. They are usually found in deeper water than butterflies – at least fifty feet, which probably explains the need for brighter colours to be seen in the dimness.

Angels are easily distinguished from butterflies by the bony spike which projects backwards half an inch or so from the gill-plate. This spike is useless as a weapon. It seems to be used rather as a means of locking the fish in a crevice so that it cannot be pulled out backwards.

Little is known of the mating of angels. They have kept this secret as well as their heavenly namesakes. The eggs are free-floating. The larvae are carried out to sea where the currents give them a wide distribution. At about one inch they transform into the juvenile fish and find the nearest reef. Like butterflies, adult angels pair for life and defend their territory to the death against others of the same species. Evolution has two answers to the problem of survival for juveniles in this situation. They can live in territory unlikely to be claimed by adults, as butterflies do, or evolve markings so different from the adults that they are not recognized by them as belonging to their own species. This is what happens with the majority of angels.

There is, however, no advantage to be gained from being different from the juveniles of other species, so nature has made several species which bear no resemblance as adults, but which are almost identical as juveniles. (For the convenience of aquarists she has been considerate enough to provide just sufficient differences to help in identification.) As for Cleaner Wrasses, there seems to be a recognized uniform for juvenile angels, which presumably entitles them to immunity from attack by adults. This uniform is black with circular or semicircular white markings, which become pale blue then electric blue as they near the periphery. The species whose juveniles wear this uniform are all those of the *Euxiphipops* genus and all of the genus *Pomacanthus*

Left: Blue-faced Angel *Euxiphipops xanthometapon*
Below: Juvenile Blue-ring Angel *Pomacanthus annularis*

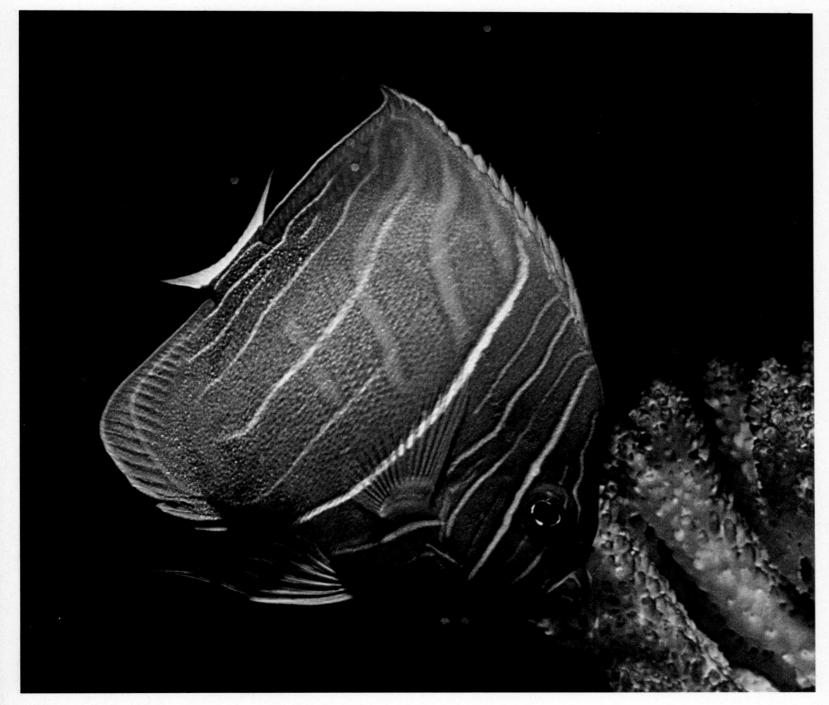

except the two Atlantic species, *P. arcuatus* and *P. paru*.

The photographs show a juvenile Blue-face Angel (*Euxiphipops xanthometapon*) from the Philippines, and the adult it will become at about four inches. The Blue-ring Angel (*Pomacanthus annularis*) from Ceylon is in the middle of its change. As an adult the vertical white marks will disappear, the diagonal lines will extend and become bright green on a light brown body.

Atlantic butterflies cannot compare with those of other tropical oceans, but angels redress the balance. Off Florida, the Caribbean Islands and Mexico are found the Rock Beauty (*Holacanthus tricolor*), vivid yellow with a large patch of jet black in the rear half, the French Angel (*Pomacanthus paru*), the juvenile, with broad yellow bands on black, the adult without the bands, but with every scale edged with yellow, the Blue Angel (*Holacanthus isabelita*), and, brightest of angels, the Queen Angel (*Holacanthus ciliaris*). The juvenile Queen Angel has several blue stripes on the body and a dark band through the eye.

Above: Queen Angel *Holacanthus ciliaris*
Right: Emperor Angel *Pomacanthus imperator*
Far right: Juvenile Blue-faced Angel *Euxiphipops xanthometapon*, above; Pakistani Butterfly, right; Lyretail Wrasse

Opinions naturally differ as to which is the most beautiful of all marine tropical fishes. My own leaning is towards the surgeons. Those who prefer a more dazzling beauty will probably choose the Emperor (*Pomacanthus imperator*) or Regal Angel (*Pygoplites diacanthus*). But of the angels my own favourite is, I think, the Majestic (*Euxiphipops nevarchus*).

Angels must not be kept with others of the same species, and must be given plenty of room in a tank with places to hide. They may need some coaxing at first, but will soon be eating everything and losing some of their shyness. I have found juveniles less shy, more eager to eat, and well able to look after themselves among larger fishes. As a bonus they afford the unique pleasure and interest of watching the transformation as they grow into a new beauty.

FAMILY ACANTHURIDAE
Surgeons
Surgeons are so called because of the retractable scalpel or flick-knife at the base of the tail. This blade is razor-sharp and up to a quarter of an inch long. By swimming alongside another fish and lashing with its tail, the surgeon can cause grievous wounds. It will do this to another fish of the same species in the aquarium, and sometimes, when established, to newly introduced fishes of other families such as butterflies and angels.

Surgeons spend much of their time browsing on algae, which forms a larger proportion of their diet than of

Left above: French Angel *Pomacanthus paru*
Left below: Rock Beauty *Holacanthus tricolor*
Below: Majestic Angel *Euxiphipops nevarchus*

any other reef fish. In the aquarium, if algae is not present in quantity, chopped spinach, parsley or lettuce will be readily taken. Surgeons are not choosy and will eat most other foods as well.

Surgeons spawn in a similar way to wrasses, a small group breaking away from a school and releasing eggs and sperm simultaneously. The eggs hatch into semi-transparent larvae. This stage is called the 'acronurus'. The larvae drift in the open sea for several weeks before returning to the reefs and changing rapidly into juveniles, usually of the same colours and markings as the adults.

Some surgeons, particularly the Regal Tang (*Paracanthurus hepatus*) and the Clown Surgeon (*Acanthurus lineatus*) are very susceptible to shock and travel badly, but most, once settled, are hardy. The Regal Tang, which has been called 'the bluest thing on earth', likes to lie inside or under the coral, dashing out for food and immediately back again. It will lie quite motionless, often on its side, for long periods. This does not indicate illness, and the fish should not be interfered with. The other surgeons are in constant movement and should have plenty of room. The Regal Tang is the smallest of the family, growing to only seven or eight inches. It is also the only species of which several may be kept together. (There are significant differences between the Pacific and Indian Ocean Regal Tangs. Those from Sri Lanka are larger, less shy, more active, and have bellies the colour of egg-yolks. Pacific Regals are the same royal blue all over.)

One of the largest of surgeons, and the most spectacular, is the Japanese, Unicorn or Lipstick Tang, (*Naso lituratus*) which grows up to eighteen inches. Japanese Tang is a bad name, since the Powder-brown Surgeon is now called *Acanthurus japonicus*. Unicorn is also a bad name. Species of the *Naso* genus are called unicorn fishes because they develop a horny projection from the forehead. But *Naso lituratus* is the one exception to this rule. *Naso lituratus* may be a unicorn without a horn, but he does have a remarkably equine head, and might have been called seahorse had that name not been preempted. The horse-like appearance is accentuated by a sculpted jawline inside the line of the gill-case, which in the adult is picked out in yellow. The adult has a further distinguishing feature in the form of long filaments extending from both tips of the tail. Perhaps I should have called *Naso lituratus* 'she'. With her lipstick, her turquoise eyeshadow, and her filamentous adornments, she is almost too selfconsciously glamorous. This species differs from the other tangs in having two non-retractable blades at the base of the tail.

Another horse-faced surgeon is the Powder-brown, with his white flashes along cheek and nose. I once obtained a Powder-brown at about one and a half inches, not long emerged from the larval stage and completely trans-

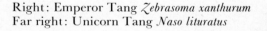

Right: Emperor Tang *Zebrasoma xanthurum*
Far right: Unicorn Tang *Naso lituratus*

parent but for a silver gutsack. I don't know how the dealer knew that he was a Powder-brown, but sure enough, over the next few months, the faint colours came, gathered strength and asserted themselves, until after about a year and grown to three inches, he looked like the photograph at the top of this page.

Equally beautiful is the popular Powder-blue Surgeon (*Acanthurus leucosternon*), plentiful in the reefs off Sri Lanka. Unfortunately, this fish does not seem to retain in captivity quite the original richness of pastel blue.

Identical with the Powder-blue and Powder-brown in shape and behaviour, but very distinctive in colour and markings is the Achilles Tang (*Acanthurus achilles*) a fish from the mid-Pacific atolls. The name derives from the Greek hero Achilles who, as a baby, was dipped by his mother in the river Styx to make him invulnerable. But she held him by the heel, which the magic water did not touch. (Hence the term 'Achilles heel' meaning the single weak spot in a man's defences.) The Trojan prince Paris knew of this, and during the seige of Troy shot Achilles in the heel with a poisoned arrow and killed him. The Achilles Tang seems wounded in the heel with that bright-red blood-drop at the base of his tail. There are other bright red markings. Body and fins are finely edged with pale blue. In the dorsal and ventral fins red suffuses the body colour, which is like no other colour I have seen in nature, half-way between maroon and brown. I look at my own four-inch Achilles as I write, his colours enhanced by Growlux lighting, and realize how badly I have failed him with my camera. He is the most handsome fish I have ever seen.

The genus *Zebrasoma* is characterized by a greater depth of body and fins, giving the fish a shape, especially when his fins are extended, quite different from other surgeons. The young are often deeper than they are long. This is most evident in the Sailfin Tang (*Z. veliferum*), but can be seen also in the Yellow Tang (*Z. flavescens*), which is most common near Hawaii, and a brighter yellow there than elsewhere in its range. The Emperor or Purple Surgeon (*Z. xanthurum*) is found only in the Indian Ocean and the Red Sea.

FAMILY BALISTIDAE
Triggers

Triggers are easily recognized by their strange rhomboid or diamond shape, as though half of them were head and the eye were in the middle of the back. This is seen at its most extreme in the genus *Rhinecanthus*. Actually in the middle of the back, just behind the eye, is the trigger from which this family gets its name. This is a long, first, dorsal spine which will lie in a groove flush with the back, or stand up at right angles. It can be locked in the upright position by the second spine so that it cannot be lowered without releasing the second spine first. It performs the same function as the gill-plate spikes in angels, enabling the trigger to wedge itself in a crevice from which it cannot then be pulled out.

Some triggers, including all the species pictured here, have a rasp at the base of the tail which is used for attack as the surgeon uses his tail-blade.

Triggers have strong teeth, and the distance between mouth and eye helps them to attack urchins and spiny star-fishes without damaging themselves. The spines of the sea urchin are sharp, poisonous, mobile, and over a foot long, but they present little problem to the trigger. He carefully takes hold of the tip of one of the longest spines and pulls the urchin over. Then he dashes round to rip into the unprotected underside before the urchin has

Below: Yellow Tang *Zebrasoma flavescens*
Top left: Powder-brown Surgeon
Acanthurus japonicus
Centre left: Achilles Tang *Acanthurus achilles*
Bottom left: Powder-blue Surgeon
Acanthurus leucosternon

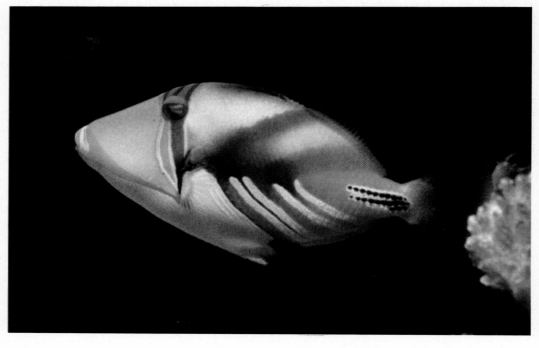

time to right itself. Alternatively, he may choose to blow the urchin over with a jet of water. If these methods do not work he has yet another in reserve. Picking up the urchin by the tip of a spine, the trigger tows him towards the surface, lets go, dives beneath it as it drifts down and attacks from below before it reaches the bottom. These same methods can be employed with equal success against the Crown of Thorns Starfish. The introduction of large numbers of triggers and puffers (the only other fish to prey on them) has been considered as a means of controlling these starfishes in the Great Barrier Reef, parts of which they have overrun and are laying waste.

Triggers spawn in large pits in the sand, about a yard across. Here they watch over and fan the eggs, savagely attacking any trespasser, including divers.

Triggers are fairly popular because of their hardiness and odd beauty, and also because they are 'personalities', becoming very tame and learning tricks. But there are several disadvantages in keeping triggers in the home aquarium. They eat a great deal of almost anything, leaving little for their tank mates. They grow fast and go on growing. Some species reach two feet in the wild. They can be very aggressive, though there are differences here not only between species but even between individuals. The Green Trigger (*Odonus niger*) seems to be the most consistently peaceful. I once saw a black trigger (*Melichthys* spp.), foiled by the dealer in its attempt to demolish a heater, turn in its frustration and take a neat half-moon out of the throat of the nearest fish. This happened to be a Pinnatus Batfish which slowly keeled over and sank – very dead.

You will never reach agreement with a trigger about the layout of your tank. He will carry pieces of coral much larger than himself industriously to the site of his choice, and excavate large trenches in the gravel.

Possibly the most famous, and certainly the most conspicuous of all marine tropicals is the Clown Trigger (*Balistoides niger*, formerly *conspicillum*). The first specimen to reach Europe alive was brought from Ceylon in 1953 and sold in Frankfurt for £260 ($650). Now they can be bought for a tenth of that. Most triggers are imported as juveniles, but the juvenile

Clown Triggers do not return to the reefs until they are several inches long. I have never seen a specimen smaller than this one (left), which was four inches. One would really need to keep such a fish alone in a very large tank with no moveable decor. I prefer to leave it to the public aquariums.

The Orange-striped Trigger (*Balistapus undulatus*) is often available quite small, but does not stay that way for very long. Unfortunately it does not develop its superb adult coloration until it is very large. The green body colour we see in this three-inch juvenile becomes purple, the orange stripes become brighter and those on the face are replaced by orange spots.

Perhaps the best trigger for a community tank is a juvenile *Rhinecanthus aculeatus*, which is relatively peaceable. The juvenile has the same markings as the adult. It is difficult to imagine how these markings could have been acquired other than by the brush strokes of a modern painter – hence the name Picasso Triggerfish.

The closely related filefishes are smaller and vegetarian, and are therefore more suitable for community tanks.

FAMILY CANTHIGASTERIDAE
Sharp-nosed Puffers

There is only one genus of sharp-nosed puffer, and one of these species is the strangely-shaped Saddled Puffer (*Canthigaster valentini*).

These small fishes have the ability to inflate themselves with water or air until they are spherical. This understandably deters predators from swallowing them. Filipino children frequently use them as footballs on the beach. The long snouts end in strong teeth capable of crushing shells and coral (and biting fingers). They have neither scales nor pelvic fins.

Apart from a tendency to nip the fins of other fishes, they are good aquarium fishes, disease-resistant and eat whatever is offered.

FAMILY OSTRACIONTIDAE
Boxfishes

The boxfishes are distinguished by the hard box-like carapace which serves both for skeleton and armour. Some, like the little *Ostracion cubicus*, are almost exactly cubic; some, the cowfishes (genus *Lactoria*) have long horns; and others have several spiky projections like the Thornback or

Top left: Orange-striped Trigger *Balistopus undulatus*
Centre left: Clown Trigger *Balistoides niger*
Bottom: Picasso Trigger *Rhinecanthus aculeatus*
Above: Puffer *Canthigaster valentini*

Hovercraft Boxfish (*Tetrasomus gibbosus*). There are holes in the box for the eyes, mouth, gills, anus and fins. The fins are small and transparent so that the box has no visible means of support as it sails slowly and rather comically along.

Boxfishes are intelligent and develop many quaint habits in the aquarium, such as spitting a considerable distance to attract attention. Their mouths are so small that they are obliged to suck in their food like spaghetti. They have no enemies since they must be as appetizing as old boot soles.

Some boxfishes exude a toxic foam when frightened. They are not immune to this themselves, and many a boxfish dead on arrival has poisoned itself in the bag. Before you leave the shop, check that there are no surface bubbles in the bag. If there are, get the dealer to change the water. The fish is unable to repeat the emission immediately.

Boxfishes are easy to feed, hardy, peaceful and tame.

FAMILY SYNGNATHIDAE
Seahorses

Even stranger than the boxfishes, but sharing with them the carapace or external skeleton, are the seahorses known at least since Roman times, and probably the only marine tropical fish which can be identified by everybody. Its quaint shape has fixed it in the popular imagination. It shares the characteristics of several very different animals, and has some uniquely its own. The head is so horse-like (and is carried so like a horse's, since the seahorse swims upright with its head at right angles) that it is disconcerting to find the chest leading not to legs but to a long prehensile tail like that of no other fish, but very like that of some reptiles and tree-dwelling mammals. The whole body is armour-plated and ridged, with many protruberances. It is so rigid that the fish has no need of an internal skeleton. This again is a feature more common in other animal classes, in insects, for example, and the independent eyes are like those of lizards.

The seahorse has only one fin, the dorsal. It moves slowly, with unshakeable dignity, as though in another dimension of time. It looks more like a brooch than a living creature, and this, sadly, is what many become.

But the most amazing characteristic, unique not only among fishes, but in the whole animal kingdom, is the fact that it is the male which becomes pregnant and gives birth. In that case, one might ask, why not call it the female? But it is the female which produces the eggs, the male the sperm. At mating the seahorses wind round each other and the female injects her eggs through a tube into the male's brood pouch. There they incubate for several weeks until, a few at a time over several days, hundreds of perfect miniature seahorses emerge. Many attach themselves to the father as he lies exhausted by this protracted labour. I am at a loss to know why the seahorse has not been chosen as the emblem of the Women's Liberation Movement.

There are several species of seahorses not differing very much from each other. The most frequently offered for sale in Europe is the Oceanic Seahorse (*Hippocampus kuda*). Specimens may be black, brown, yellow, white, or, occasionally, red. These are colour phases, not permanent differences, and they may change colour in a short time.

Seahorses live where warm currents bring a steady stream of plankton to them. Anchored by their tails to the bottom growth they reach out and suck in small creatures through their pipette-like snouts. They will eat nothing but live food (or what they take to be alive) of exactly the right size, and are consequently difficult to feed in captivity, (small live prawns are excellent if available). Newly hatched brine shrimp are too small except for the Dwarf Seahorse (*H. zosterae*), and few aquarists can raise brine shrimp to adult size. Sometimes they will take daphnia and glassworm. Baby Guppies or other livebearers are often suggested, but these tend to swim on the surface and in taking them the seahorses swallow air, which they are unable to expel, and which eventually kills them. Frozen brine or mysis shrimps offer a new hope. A block of frozen shrimps floated on the surface gradually releases shrimps which sink, are caught in the filter current and taken by the seahorses.

Top left: Boxfish *Ostracion cubicus*
Bottom: Hovercraft Boxfish *Tetrasomus gibbosus*
Right: Seahorse *Hippocampus kuda*

Since they cannot compete with other fishes for food, seahorses must have a tank to themselves, perhaps with invertebrates, or a few, gentle, slow-moving fishes, such as clowns.

FAMILY POMADASYIDAE
Grunts

Grunts are so called because of the noise they make by grinding their teeth together. They are usually to be seen in large numbers around the reefs by day, scattering at night to forage for invertebrates.

Grunts of the genus *Gaterin* are known as 'sweetlips' because their lips are rather thick. The young sweetlips has an odd way of swimming, the large pectorals doing all the work, as if a small boy were trying to manoeuvre a large rowing boat with oars too big for him.

The juvenile Polka-dot Grunt or Clown Sweetlips (*Gaterin chaetodonoides*) has large white dots on a brown background. As it grows, small brown dots appear in the centre of the white ones which extend and run together until in the adult the colour scheme

becomes completely reversed.

Polka-dot Grunts make very attractive aquarium inmates, though large specimens can be bullies. They will grow to three feet in the wild, but modify their growth in the aquarium, despite eating a great deal.

FAMILY HOLOCENTRIDAE
Squirrelfishes

The large eyes which are the primary feature of squirrelfishes indicate that they are nocturnal. Prolonged exposure to bright aquarium lighting is distressing to them and they must be provided with shaded areas. Red coloration also seems to be common among nocturnal species, though at a depth of thirty or forty feet red cannot be seen, and they might just as well be grey or black.

Squirrelfishes grow to several inches. Their diet is mainly of crustaceans. They eat voraciously in captivity, especially if fed in the evening. But they cannot be trusted with small fishes such as damsels.

Within a genus, the differences between species are very small, so

Left: Polka Dot Grunt *Gaterin chaetodonoides*
Above: Squirrelfishes *Myripristis* sp.
Below: Soldierfish *Adioryx* sp.

that exact identification, especially from photographs, is very difficult. Squirrelfishes of the genus *Myripristis* (also known as soldierfishes) are likely to be found in groups or schools, those of the genus *Adioryx* singly or in pairs. Squirrelfishes are considered to be a delicacy in many parts of the world, particularly in Hawaii.

FAMILY APOGONIDAE
Cardinals
Cardinals are not necessarily always red, as their name suggests. They are small, shy fishes, spending much of their time in the aquarium quite

Left: Mandarin Fish *Synchiropus splendidus*
Below: Cardinal *Apogon nematopterus*
Right: Round Batfish *Platax orbicularis*

motionless, as if suspended, not far from a hiding place, darting forward at feeding time to swallow some sizeable morsels with their large mouths.

In the reef many species move about in enormous shoals and some have a symbiosis with the sea-urchin, living among its spines. Cardinals occasionally incubate their eggs in their mouths.

They are found in a wide variety of habitats, some in shallow water, others in deep, some in salt water, others in brackish or even freshwater.

FAMILY CALLIONYMIDAE
Dragonets
The dragonets are small fishes whose markings remind one of fine oriental silks – hence the name Mandarin Fish (*Synchiropus splendidus*). They are bottom-dwelling fishes, highly territorial, with greater differences than are usual in marine fishes between the sexes. In the male the first two dorsal rays are highly extended, as in cichlids.

Mandarin Fishes are fairly rare and consequently expensive, but seem to do well in the aquarium if kept singly. Two males will fight to the death.

FAMILY GRAMMIDAE
Grammas
This beauty from the Caribbean area, the Royal Gramma (*Gramma loreto*) is a full-grown specimen of about three inches. Grammas have a habit of swimming upside-down in caves or under ledges which makes them hard to catch and expensive. They are very aggressive with other grammas and not easily encouraged to start eating in captivity, and are thus not recommended for the beginner.

FAMILY PLATACIDAE
Batfishes
The young Round Batfish (*Platax orbicularis*) looks very like a bat, though a less fanciful name would be leaf-fish, for batfishes drift with the surface currents among the dead mangrove leaves and are virtually indistinguishable from them. As an adult he will have lost his beautiful russet colour and become a dirty brownish-grey.

The two other species of batfishes, *Platax teira* and *Platax pinnatus* have even more elongated fins, which make them look more like boomerangs than bats, especially as juveniles. The fins grow, initially, much faster than the body, but the body later catches up, so

that the adult *P. orbicularis* is quite round, as his name implies, while the Long-finned Batfish (*P. teira*) whose height as a juvenile is several times its length, seems, as an adult, still to be wearing its juvenile fins, now much too small. Only *P. pinnatus* retains some of the majesty of his juvenile height and colouring. He has an orange rim all round which makes him look as though silhouetted against a bright orange light concealed behind him. The first photograph I saw I had assumed to have been achieved with trick lighting; I was amazed, when I saw a live specimen, to find that nothing had been added to nature. *P. pinnatus* is the most dignified of all fishes.

All the batfishes eat literally anything in the wild. The Round Batfish retains that habit in captivity, growing an inch a month, and vies with *Pterois volitans* (one of the scorpions) for the title of hardiest marine tropical fish; but the other two species are loth to eat at all in the aquarium, especially *P. pinnatus*, which gives the impression that even to glance at food would be altogether beneath its dignity. Round Batfishes can be bought as babies but *P. pinnatus* is rarely less than six inches high.

Batfishes are very tame. They will take food from the fingers (as will many marines), and do not seem to mind being tickled. But they are quite defenceless and must on no account be kept with potentially aggressive fishes, such as triggers, puffers, or even the larger damsels.

Left: Pinnatus Batfish *Platax pinnatus*
Above: Royal Gramma *Gramma loreto*

FAMILY SCORPAENIDAE
Scorpions

The scorpion is also sometimes known as the dragon-fish, the lion-fish, the turkey-fish and the fire-fish. He is adapted to bottom-living, splendidly camouflaged, his long pectoral rays floating like the fronds of a plant, his face disguised by grotesque flaps of skin, his body shape broken by stripes. He has only to sit still on the bottom, or suspended on a rock and his prey will usually come to him. He swims very slowly, rather floats than swims, over any distance, but over the first few inches he is very fast, with all the leverage a single stroke of his pectorals can give him. A lunge, a snap and a gulp and the unsuspecting shrimp or small fish has become a bulge in the

scorpion's belly. If he needs to go hunting, he can gently shepherd his prey into a dead end, using his wings like nets. Nor is his slowness any disadvantage where predators are concerned. When danger threatens he spreads his fins, puts his head down, and ripples his dorsal rays, presenting a fearsome appearance. If this should not deter the aggressor, those rays are loaded with deadly poison.

There is some danger in keeping scorpions. Not that they ever use their poison spines to attack – in fact they carefully collapse them when another non-aggressive fish swims near – but that the aquarist might thrust his fingers onto the spines when moving something on the bottom of the tank. If this happens, the victim must be

Left: *Pterois volitans*
Above: *Dendrochirus zebra*

rushed to hospital at once for injections. Meanwhile, brandy will help.

The other main disadvantage of scorpions is that they grow fast and cannot be kept for long with small fishes such as clowns and damsels (Cleaner Wrasses are quite safe with them). The best policy is to trade your scorpions in the week before he swallows his first damsel. In practice, it is more likely to be the week after.

There are two genera of scorpions, *Pterois* and *Dendrochirus*. The most obvious difference is that the latter have pectoral rays connected for most of their length by membranes, which can be clearly seen in this photograph of *Dendrochirus zebra*.

Luckily, the most spectacular scorpion, with the longest wings, *Pterois*

volitans, is also the commonest and easiest to keep. There is no hardier fish. For the first few days it may be necessary to tempt him with live shrimps, baby guppies or earthworms, but it will not take him long to learn that whatever you drop into the tank is food. They are great characters and will often spit jets of water into your face if they think you are too slow with the next course.

Other scorpions take longer to extend their diet beyond live foods, and some, including the handsome *Pterois radiata* rarely do so.

AQUARIUM PHOTOGRAPHY
Aquarium photography is not difficult given the right equipment – a good single-lens reflex camera and an elec-

tronic flash gun with extension lead. Most of the photographs in this book were taken with a Pentax 35 mm. camera on Agfa CT18 film.

Do not attempt to illuminate from the front; this results in almost inevitable glare or reflection from the front glass, and in any case produces a very unnatural effect with fishes staring glassy-eyed and throwing black shadows. Place the flash gun on the cover-glass, at the front, over the part of the tank where you intend to take your photographs. If you want a specific background or if you know the fish you want will stay put, you can use a tripod, but it is not really necessary as the speed of the flash obviates the risk of camera shake. If the camera is hand-held you must resist the temp-

Below: *Pterois volitans*

tation to follow fishes out of the range of the flash. If you want to photograph a whole aquarium or a large section of it you will need more than one flash gun. An adaptor can be bought very cheaply which enables you to fire two or three guns simultaneously.

If the flash gun is at the front of the cover-glass and is not tilted, the background will be black. If you want the decor behind the fish to show, either use a second flash-gun or move the gun to the middle of the cover-glass and wait until the fish goes to the back of the tank. If your subject is in front of the flash it will become a silhouette. If it is directly underneath, its lower half will be in deep shadow. Ideally the gun should be positioned four to six inches in front of the subject.

Most flash exposure guides go down only to a metre, but in any case they do not apply when the lighting is through water. By keeping a record of all your exposures you will soon be able to calculate exactly the right exposure for your own tanks. As a rough guide, using 50 ASA film, the following exposures will be needed. If the flash-to-subject distance is less than eight inches f22 (if your camera does not have f22, use f16 and put a white handkerchief under the flash-gun); eight–twelve inches f16; twelve–eighteen inches f11; eighteen–twenty-four inches f8. With 100–125 ASA film use one stop less.

Most single-lens reflex cameras will focus down to eighteen inches, which is near enough for the larger fishes or a school of small ones. To move in closer you will need automatic extension rings. Rings simply increase the distance between the lens and the film, which has an enlarging effect. Rings are sold in sets of three. Remember to allow half-a-stop additional exposure when the small ring is used; one stop for the middle ring and $1\frac{1}{2}$ stops for the large.

Before you start a photographic session clean the inside of the front glass, which is almost bound to have some algae even if this is not evident at a distance. Also turn off all aeration or every tiny bubble in the water will be brightly illuminated by the flash.

Finally, remember that however good your equipment and technique you will not get good results without perfect specimens. The camera cannot lie.

Bibliography

Axelrod and Others, *Exotic Tropical Fishes*, Bailey Bros. 1962

Axelrod and Emmens, *Exotic Marine Fishes*, Tropical Fish Hobbyist, New Jersey 1971

Axelrod and Vorderwinkler, *Encyclopaedia of Tropical Fishes*, T.F.H. 1961, Ward Lock 1963

Burgess and Axelrod, *Pacific Marine Fishes* 1–5, T.F.H. 1972–5

Butterfield, *The Coral Reef*, Hamlyn 1964

Cox, *Tropical Marine Aquaria*, Hamlyn 1971

Cust and Cox, *Tropical Aquarium Fishes – Freshwater and Marine*, Hamlyn 1972

Cust and Bird, *Tropical Freshwater Aquaria*, Hamlyn 1970

Dutta, *Tropical Fish*, Octopus 1972

Fricke, *The Coral Seas*, Thames and Hudson, 1973

Gilbert Legge, *The Complete Aquarist's Guide to Freshwater Tropical Fishes*, Ward Lock 1970

Gohm, *Tropical Fish*, Hamlyn 1970

de Graff, *Marine Aquarium Guide*, Pet Library, 1974

von Hentig, *Coral World*, B.B.C. 1973

Hervey and Hems, *A Guide to Freshwater Aquarium Fishes*, Hamlyn 1973

Innes, *Exotic Aquarium Fishes*, Innes Publications, 1959

Randall, *Caribbean Reef Fishes*, T.F.H. 1968

Sterba, *Freshwater Fishes of the World*, Studio Vista 1964

Wickler, *The Marine Aquarium*, Studio Vista 1967

Index

Page numbers that appear in *italics* refer to captions to illustrations.

Acknowledgments

The author would like to express his gratitude to all the aquarists who have allowed him to photograph their fishes:
Oceanarium, Cleveleys; Q.S.S. Aquatics, Bradford; Aquascope, Blackburn; and to members of the Blackburn Water-life Society. The author's remaining photographs were taken in his own tanks.

The publishers would like to thank the following individuals and organizations for their kind permission to reproduce the photographs in this book:

Biofotos: 1, 6–7, 10, 16–17, 20, 21, 42, 44, 57; Bruce Coleman Ltd: Jane Burton 2–3; Jacana Agence de Presse: 12–13, 14, 19, 27, 35, 37, 39, 45, 49, 50 above, 63, 77, 88, below; Keith Sagar: 4–5, 7 below, 8, 9, 11, 15, 18, 22–25, 26, 28–34, 36, 38, 40, 41, 46–48, 50 below, 51–56, 58–62, 64, 76, 78–87, 88 above, 89–95

First published 1976 by
Octopus Books Limited
59 Grosvenor Street, London W.1

ISBN 0 7064 0291 X

© 1976 Octopus Books Limited

Distributed in USA by
Crescent Books
a division of Crown Publishers Inc
419 Park Avenue South
New York, N.Y. 10016

Produced by Mandarin Publishers Limited
22a Westlands Road, Quarry Bay,
Hong Kong

Printed in Hong Kong